Clifford Richardson

Foods and food adulterants

Part Second: Spices and Condiments

Clifford Richardson

Foods and food adulterants
Part Second: Spices and Condiments

ISBN/EAN: 9783337201135

Printed in Europe, USA, Canada, Australia, Japan

Cover: Foto ©Andreas Hilbeck / pixelio.de

More available books at **www.hansebooks.com**

U. S. DEPARTMENT OF AGRICULTURE.

DIVISION OF CHEMISTRY.

BULLETIN No. 13.

FOODS

AND

FOOD ADULTERANTS.

BY DIRECTION OF

THE COMMISSIONER OF AGRICULTURE.

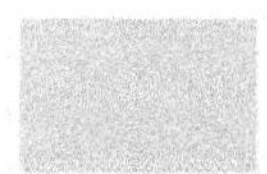

PART SECOND:

SPICES AND CONDIMENTS.

BY

CLIFFORD RICHARDSON.

WASHINGTON:
GOVERNMENT PRINTING OFFICE.
1887.

[BULLETIN NO. 13.]

PART 2.—SPICES AND CONDIMENTS.

U. S. DEPARTMENT OF AGRICULTURE,
DIVISION OF CHEMISTRY,
Washington, D. C., March 15, 1887.

SIR: Having been directed by you to make an examination of the adulteration of spice and condiments, I have been engaged at different times during the past year upon the subject, and with some aid from the assistants in the laboratory in performing the chemical determinations have prepared the following report, which forms part 2 of Bulletin No. 13 of this Division. It has been my endeavor to collect all the available information in regard to the extent and character of this adulteration in all parts of the world, and to describe for the benefit of investigators the means to be employed for its detection. More particularly I have entered into an examination of the spices and condiments found in the markets of Washington and Balitimore, and have tested with them the methods of investigation which are described.

It has seemed appropriate to divide the report into two parts, the first being devoted to a popular exposition of the origin of the spices and the means employed for their adulteration, while the second contains a more extended technical discussion of the subject and of the results of analysis, both microscopical and chemical, and the methods which have been proposed by recent authorities for the detection of sophistication. I have been assisted in the chemical work by Messrs. Knorr, Trescot, and Fake, assistants in the laboratory of the Division, who have completed a large portion of the determinations under my supervision, and I am indebted to Dr. Battershall, of New York, for the privilege of examining the advanced sheets of his work on food adulteration.

To the standard authorities, Hassall, Koenig, Schimper, and others, I owe much for the information derived from them, although their work is not entirely applicable in this country, and I have copied from Schimper some of his diagramatic drawings of the spices, which, although extremely deceptive to the beginner, may in their proper way be made of value for reference. Other sources of information I have acknowledged in the body of the report.

The amount of adulteration which has been detected is extremely large and of a nature which apparently arouses but little prejudice on the part of the consumer, being free from associations of uncleanliness. Could only a portion of the unfortunate dislike for oleomargarine be directed toward the spices, the result would be that much wasted energy would be turned into a profitable channel. The necessity for some means for the suppression of the present universal sophistication of spices and condiments seems urgent.

Very respectfully,

CLIFFORD RICHARDSON.

Dr. H. W. WILEY.

SPICES AND CONDIMENTS.

PART I.

Under this head are included substances which while not in themselves foods serve to render the latter more palatable, and to stimulate digestion. They occupy an important position in the diet of the human race, and are largely subject to adulteration or sophistication. Among the more common are: Peppers of various kinds, mustard, cloves, cinnamon, cassia, allspice or pimento, nutmeg, mace, ginger.

These substances are so often and seriously adulterated because it is readily accomplished, owing to the custom of putting them on the market in a ground condition, which prevents the recognition of quality from mere appearance, and because so many cheap substitutes or diluents are readily found which resemble the real article. In addition, the demand on the part of the poorer classes for the cheapest possible supply and the competition brought about by this demand in the trade has, owing to general high prices attached to most of the spices of good quality, fostered and extended the practice.

At the present time in several of our largest cities the price to be paid for a spice is named by the retail dealer, and he is then furnished from the spice-mill with a mixture containing the largest amount of pure material which can be supplied for the money, the necessary weight being made up of diluents of some cheap but harmless substance, different grades being distinguished by one firm as pure, extra, No. 1, and superior, none of which are pure and many of which are mere variation in labels with none in quality. As examples, the fact that a New York firm, it is understood, in a short time used and put upon the market in their spices more than 5,000 pounds of cocoanut shells, and the following quotations from a journal devoted to spice milling show how universal and open the custom has become. On a prominent page is found:

"All necessary information for spice manufacturing supplied."

Attention should be paid to the use of the word manufacturing.

Then the following advertisements appear, from which the names have been stricken out:

——— ———

MANUFACTURER OF

SPICES, SPICE MIXTURES, AND MUSTARDS,

181 ——— *Street, N. Y.*

Goods made to order for Wholesale Grocers and Druggists; also, Grinding done for Jobbers who pack their own Goods.

Spice Mixtures and Cayenne Pepper a Specialty.

——— ———,

17 ——— STREET, NEW YORK,

MANUFACTURER OF

ALL KINDS OF SPICE MIXTURES.

My celebrated brand of P. D. Pepper is superior to any made.

Samples sent on application. Goods shipped to all parts of the United States. Spice mixtures a specialty. Spices ground for the trade. We are the Inventors of Suction Coolers.

The firms advertising do not hesitate to call themselves manufacturers instead of millers.

It is easy to see how difficult it must be to bring this state of things to an end without some governmental action, it being improbable that by any means of agreement among themselves the grinders of spices could unite in doing away with the practice, or that any education of the masses will teach them to refuse to purchase a ground spice at a price which is far below that of the unground article. This alone, the relation between the prices of ground and unground spices, is often sufficient to point out the fact that a ground spice must be largely diluted, and, on the other hand, when purchasing from a reliable dealer, a slight increase in cost over that of the spice in its original form is fair evidence of the purity of the powder. Those who desire pure ground spices can almost always obtain them by paying their value. They are by no means uncommon in the market, but as long as there are those who do not know that it is for their interest to buy the best, rather than a cheap article on account of its low price, such people must suffer or be protected by legal enactments which shall prevent and prohibit the existence of such mixtures. Until this is done the supply of a demand which certainly exists may be considered to be, at the least, justifiable on the part of the spice millers, and education of those ignorant of the state of the trade must be the preliminary to legislation upon the subject. When proper legislation has found a place on the statute-books the manufacturers will find themselves in a position where, without detriment to themselves, they can all unite in giving up the practice. Under the laws for the prevention of the adulteration of foods which have been in operation in Germany, England, France, Canada, and a few of our States, during a longer or shorter period of time, a large share of attention has been given to the adulteration of spices and condiments and the means of detecting them. Fortunately the latter are not difficult, and the results have been an awakening of the communities in these countries to an appreciation of the advantages of pure spices and the placing of the method of detection on a more certain basis.

EXPERIENCE IN COUNTRIES HAVING PUBLIC ANALYSTS.

In England the public mind had been so far educated by the publications of private investigators, such as Hassall, that in 1860 laws were passed for the prevention of the adulteration of food and drink. These have been modified and repealed, so that the present law dates from 1875 and amendments of 1879. Unfortunately there is no Government report, of which we are aware, upon the results of the scientific work done by those employed under the act, and we are indebted to the Society of Public Analysts for a large portion of the information which is at our disposal in regard to adulteration in England. We have also in the publications of Hassal, Blyth, and Allen volumes which give the most recent scientific data as to the best methods for the detection of adulteration, and illustrations of the forms in which foreign matter occurs. On Dr. Hassall's work is founded many of our present methods of examining foods microscopically, and especially spices and condiments. In the Analyst, the publication of the Society of Public Analysts, will be found among the proceedings of the society, in papers of individuals, and in reports of prosecutions, much information in regard to the status of adulteration in England during the last eleven years, including the material used for adulteration of spices and the means of detecting it. The lack of an official publication of the results of all that has been done in regard to particular samples and of the methods employed for their examination is, however, much to be regretted. There is the same difficulty in Germany. The law of the Empire of 1881 provides for the prevention of the adulteration of the substances which we have under consideration, but no reports on the execution of the law or of the results, scientific or otherwise, have been made available to us. Much, however, has been published in the German technical and scientific journals on the methods of detecting adulterants, which is of the greatest value.

In France, the laboratory of the prefecture of police of Paris, which has control of the investigation of the food supplies of that city, makes an elaborate report annually, of which, however, but a small portion is devoted to spices, although they are recognized as being largely adulterated, pepper, for example, being mixed to an astonishing extent with ground olive stones. Other cities of France have municipal laboratories whose reports, if any there are, have not reached us.

In this country Canada makes a much better statement of the results which have followed the enforcement of the adulteration-of-food act of 1876 than is done anywhere else. The commissioner of inland revenue has published annually for eight or ten years a statement showing the entire number of samples analyzed, the persons supplying them, and their composition and adulterants. Spices occupy a prominent position in the reports, and a collation of the results of the investigations of the several public analysts is of interest. In 1878, when the reports first become available to us for reference, the summary of the spices analyzed showed:

Articles.	Unadulterated.	Adulterated.	Per cent. adulterated.
Allspice	1	11	92.5
Cassia	2	2	50.0
Cloves	3	15	83.3
Cinnamon	3	6	66.6
Ginger	5	8	61.5
Mustard	....	38	100.0
Pepper	12	28	70.0

This enormous amount of adulteration, amounting to nearly a universal custom, was followed in 1879 by a similar report:

Articles.	Unadulterated.	Adulterated.	Per cent. adulterated.
Allspice	6	10	62.5
Cassia	....	1	....
Cloves	7	9	56.2
Cinnamon	3	16	84.2
Ginger	5	6	55.5
Mace	5	1	16.6
Mustard	3	....	....
Pepper	22	21	48.8

In 1880 there were reported as the results of the public analysts' work:

Articles.	Unadulterated.	Adulterated.	Per cent. adulterated.
Allspice	15	6	31.6
Cloves	12	10	45.5
Cinnamon	6	16	72.7
Ginger	9	8	47.1
Mustard	....	16	100.0
Pepper	21	18	42.9

There is a very slight improvement apparent, but it must be remembered that in examinations of this description the specimens selected are always of a suspicious nature, those which are already known to be pure being omitted, so that year by year the list of brands which are excluded from examination increases.

In 1881 and the following years results were tabulated as follows:

Articles.	1881.		1882.		1883.		1884.		1885.	
	Genuine.	Adulterated.	Genuine.	Adulterated.	Genuine.	Adulterated.	Genuine.	Adulterated.	Genuine.	Adulterated.
Allspice	8	17	......	......	......	......	......	......	......	......
Cloves	6	7	......	......	......	......	......	......	12	10
Cinnamon or cassia	12	12	......	......	......	......	......	......	......	......
Ginger	7	5	7	16	......	......	......	......	37	29
Mace	1	1	......	......	......	......	......	......	......	......
Mustard	2	2	......	......	......	......	......	......	11	*39
Nutmeg	1	......	......	......	......	......	......	......	......	......
Pepper	16	29	14	28	......	......	......	......	31	29
Cayenne	......	......	......	......	......	......	......	......	13	11
Total	53	73	31	32	48	86	38	112	103	118

* Many labeled mixtures.

It is seen that several years after the enactment of the law adulteration of spices is as enormous as at first. This, however, seems to arise largely from lack of prosecution and non enforcement of the law. Of the occurrence of adulterants in spices, the chief analyst says, in his report for 1885:

During the year considerable attention was paid to spices and condiments. Viewing the fact that in the past a very large amount of adulteration had been reported as prevailing in these substances, and with a view to ascertaining whether the adulteration was practiced by the manufacturers or by the dealers, a systematic visitation was made of all the spice grinders in the Dominion (or of all that could be recognized as such), and their factories and stores were inspected under sections 7 and 8 with the results as shown in the appendix.

The examination of nineteen samples of ground cinnamon resulted in finding seven genuine; four to consist of a substitution of cassia; one was adulterated with cassia, and six with other inert matter; one consisted of cassia adulterated with foreign vegetable matter.

Of ground cloves, twenty-two samples were examined. Twelve proved to be pure and ten adulterated, the adulterant chiefly used being clove stems, pea-meal, roasted and ground cocoanut shells.

Of sixty-six samples of ground ginger, twenty-nine were reported as being adulterated, almost exclusively with wheat flour, non-injurious to health, doubtless; but unless the purchaser be duly warned of the nature of the compound his pocket would be seriously prejudiced, if not injured, as this sophistication was practiced to the extent of from 10 to 15 to from 25 to 40 per cent., the pungency being imparted by the judicious admixture of cayenne pepper.

Fifty samples of mustard were examined, and many of these were properly sold as "compound" or mixtures, but one of the worst samples was sold with a label guaranteeing it to be "ground from finest English seed, and free from adulteration." Of the fifty samples, nine were reported genuine, two of excellent quality, and thirty-nine were all, more or less, admixtures of mustard seed or mustard cake (from which the natural fixed oil had been expressed) with wheat flour and turmeric, and, in some cases, with corn-starch or bean meal, in varying proportions, up to as high as 50 or even 60 per cent. It was formerly contended that the addition of wheat flour or other inert matter was a necessity, to give the ground mustard keeping qualities and make the condiment palatable by softening its natural acidity. But the most reputable manufacturers have demonstrated the fallacy of this contention by the production of an absolutely pure mustard, which has received public acceptance and appreciation, and two, at least, of our home manufacturers are happily following in their steps. It is a question yet to be decided how far the use of mustard cake, deprived of the natural fixed oil, is permissible in the manufacture of this condiment. Dr. Ellis' observations on this matter are very much to the point, and have received confirmation by similar experiments in my laboratory, and doubtless when next the analysts meet in conference this question will be settled in a manner favorable to the use of mustard cake.

Twenty-four samples of cayenne pepper were examined, of which fourteen were reported adulterated, but three of these were appealed to the judgment of the chief analyst, and the decision of the public analysts was not sustained, as will be seen on reference to "appeal cases." The remaining ten were reported adulterated with wheat flour and colored earth, in one case to the extent of 50 per cent. The other ten samples were reported unadulterated, save one, which was doubtful, it apparently having been artificially dressed with a fixed oil.

Sixty samples of ground pepper, black and white, were examined, of which thirty-one are reported as unadulterated, one doubtful, and twenty-eight all more or less adulterated—the generality of them to the extent of from 10 per cent. to 20 per cent., but the more flagrant cases from 30 up to even 75 per cent. in one case. The adulterant is chiefly farinaceous matter, also mustard husk, pepper hulls, clay, sand, and, not the least conspicuous, *ground cocoanut shells*—doubtless an innocent admixture, so far as health is concerned, but decidedly not a material of a character to improve the flavor or value of the pepper as a condiment.

As stated, these samples of spices were all obtained from either the actual producer or wholesale distributers; and the results prove that whether or not the retail vender still further "improves" his spices, &c., before retailing them, his demand for a cheap, adulterated article is amply provided for by the manufacturing dealer.

For the most part, the producers of these sophisticated goods expressed themselves anxious for the enforcement of the law, that, if sold, they should be distinctly labeled as impure. Some, on the other hand, contended that the public was benefited by a slight admixture—that a really better article could be supplied at a lower price if the finest and freshest spices were ground with an admixture of inert matter, than a thoroughly pure article, but ground from old or perished spices—a specious contention, utterly untenable in the true interests of the public.

But have not the producers of these sophistications some justification; is not the supply of a demand which, undoubtedly, has existed, a justifiable enterprise, whatever that demand may be, so long as it is within the law? Ignorance does, undoubtedly, demand cheapness, and a demand thus ignorantly made is only too surely supplied, and hence the need for costly legislation to protect an ignorant and thoughtless public against itself, for it does demand the very goods which the analyst must condemn and the vender be prosecuted and fined for selling, whereas the public's reckless ignorance is the chief cause, and should suffer some measure of the penalty. It is time that through the operation of this act such ignorance should be cleared away, and the public be enlightened and awakened to its own true interests.

These remarks apply equally well to much of the spices sold in the United States. Massachusetts, New York, New Jersey, and Michigan alone have laws* of any value in regard to the adulteration of food, and it is easy to see in what condition the spices and condiments sold in other parts of the country must be. In Massachusetts, where investigations under the law have been going on since 1882, it has been shown, as in other localities, that the adulterants of spices are numerous but harmless. Dr. Sharpless, in his report of 1882 upon the subject, remarks,

* See Appendix.

that he agrees with the opinion expressed by Dr. Leeds, of New Jersey, in his report of 1880 to the New Jersey State board of health, that there has been much sensational writing upon the subject. This is perhaps the case with some few writers of that stamp, but it can have done no harm, for it has not produced sufficient effect upon the public to create a demand for any purer spices, as appears from the figures of Dr. E. S. Wood in 1882, who reports in regard to the samples he examined as analyst of foods for Massachnsetts:

Articles.	Genuine.	Adulterated.	Per cent. adulterated.
Black pepper	20	44	68.75
White pepper	13	31	70.45
Red pepper	5	....	....
Mustard	29	47	61.84
Ground cloves	0	11	100.00
Cassia	0	2	100.00
Pimento	2	....	....
Ginger	1	....	....

This is nearly as serious a condition as was found in Canada, but again, in 1885, Dr. Wood reports:

Articles.	Genuine.	Adulterated.	Compounds.	Per cent. adulterated.
Mustard	31	37	20	64.8
Cloves	15	76	....	83.5
Cassia and cinnamon	48	26	1	36.0
Ginger	55	17	....	23.6
Allspice	30	8	....	21.1
Ground mace	9	9	....	50.0
Black pepper	6	19	3	78.6
White peper	21	39	....	65.0

The above is little or no improvement. He found the common adulterants of mustard to be flour, turmeric, and sometimes a little cayenne. Cloves suffered from extraction of the volatile oil and the addition of clove stems, allspice, burnt shells, and other cheap substances. Cassia contained ground shells and crackers; ginger was in many cases colored, and in some instances wheat and corn flour and clove stems were present. Allspice is too cheap to be often adulterated, but in eight samples mustard hulls, ground shells, clove stems, and cracker dust were found. In mace, flour and cornmeal were diluents, and for the peppers, crackers, mustard hulls, pepper dirt, powdered charcoal, rice, corn, and buckwheat.

Under the New York law of 1881, Prof. S. A. Lattimore investigated a number of spices and spice mixtures submitted to him.

Professor Lattimore's report furnishes abundant proof in support of the common impression regarding the adulteration of spices.

On the results of his examination of the commercial ground spices he comments, after giving the proportions which were found adulterated, in these words:

Articles.	Samples examined.	Adulterated.	Percentage of adulteration.
Mustard	18	12	66.6
Ginger	15	9	60.0
Allspice	27	19	70.4
Cinnamon	22	18	81.8
Cassia	7	4	57.1
Cloves	21	16	76.2
Pepper:			
Black	40	28	70.0
White	7	5	71.4
Red	10	5	50.0
Mace	8	4	50.0
Nutmeg	5	2	40.0

As the above table shows, a large proportion of them are adulterated, and that with substances presenting a certain uniformity. The spices present an inviting field for the exercise of fraudulent arts. They are almost universally sold in the form of fine powder and in opaque packages, which do not admit of easy examination on the part of the purchaser. Consequently any cheap substance which may be easily pulverized to a similar degree of fineness, and which possesses little distinctive taste or odor of its own, answers the purpose; so that the list of adulterants for this class of articles is naturally very large. The adulterations found in the samples now under consideration may be classed into four groups. First, integuments of grains of seeds, such as bran of wheat and buckwheat, hulls of mustard seed, flax seed, &c. Second, farinaceous substances of low price, such as are damaged by the accidents of transportation or long storage—such as middlings of various kinds, corn-meal, and stale ship's bread. Third, leguminous seeds, as peas and beans, which contribute largely to the profit of the spice mixer. Fourth, various articles chosen with reference to their suitableness for bringing up the mixture as nearly as possible to the required standard of color of the genuine article. Various shades, from light colors to dark browns, may be obtained by the skillful roasting of farinaceous and leguminous substances. A little turmeric goes a great way in imparting the rich yellow hue of real mustard to a pale counterfeit of wheat flour and terra alba, or the defective paleness of artificial black pepper is brought up to the desired tone by the judicious sifting in of a little finely pulverized charcoal. Enough has been already given to show that the field for sophistications of this sort is a wide one, and offers large scope for the development of inventive genius; so that each manufacturer of articles of this class would be likely to possess his own trade secrets. It will be observed that the adulterating materials just mentioned all belong to the class claimed to be harmless. In no instance has any poisonous substance been discovered. The proportion of foreign and genuine substances in the spices varies between wide limits, in some instances the former being slight; in others, the latter seemingly present in just sufficient quantity to impart faintly the requisite taste or odor. Even this small proportion of the professed article is occasionally further diminished by the substitution of other substances; as, for example, in imparting to corn-meal finely ground a pungency suggested by real ginger by the addition of a little salt and red pepper.

It is probably not so widely known as it should be that the demand for the materials for adulteration has called into existence a branch of manufacturing industry of no insignificant magnitude, having for its sole object the production of articles known as "spice mixtures" or "pepper dust." The use of "pepper dust," or, as the article is commonly designated in the technical language of the trade by its abbreviation "P. D.," is a venerable fraud.

The manufacture of "P. D." is now a regular branch of business, and the original and specific term "pepper dust" has expanded with the progress of inventive art to generic proportions, until now we have as well-known articles sold by the barrel "P. D. pepper," "P. D. ginger," "P. D. cloves," and so on through the whole aromatic list. When it is considered that these imitations, lacking only such flavoring with the genuine article as the dealer thinks necessary to make his goods sell, are sold at from three to four cents a pound, and the retail price paid by the consumer is compared with it, the strength of the temptation to engage in such practices is clearly seen. When manufacturers openly advertise themselves as assorters and renovators of merchandise, and openly propose to cleanse musty and damaged beans by a new and patented process, it is full time that its significance should be considered by the public.

From the investigations, which have been quoted, it appears that the adulterants which are met with in this country are very numerous. Under the head of spice mixtures, or "P. D.," much refuse of all descriptions is used up, and there are such changes in the character of the material from time to time as the sources of damaged material or refuse at hand may suggest. The diluents used in Baltimore and in the District of Columbia seem to be different from those in New York, and, in consequence, some of the adulterants which are mentioned most commonly in the reports from the North are not found in the spices of southern millers. While it is possible, therefore, to give a list of substances which have been used as adulterants, it is quite out of the question to say in what directions the ingenuity of spice-mixers will extend in the future. The following contaminations in the various spices have been already noted in this country:

Spices.	Adulterants.
Allspice	Spent cloves, clove stems, cracker dust, *ground shells* or charcoal, *mineral color yellow corn.*
Cayenne	*Rice flour*, salt and shipstuff, *yellow corn*, *turmeric*, and *mineral red.*
Cassia	*Ground shells* and *crackers*, *turmeric*, *minerals.*
Cinnamon	*Cassia*, peas, starch, *mustard hulls*, *turmeric*, *minerals*, *cracker dust*, *burnt shells* or charcoal.
Cloves	*Spent cloves*, *clove stems*, *minerals*, allspice, roasted shells, wheat flour, peas.
Ginger	*Cereals*, *turmeric*, *mustard hulls*, *cayenne*, peas.
Mace	Cereals or starch, buckwheat, *wild mace.*
Nutmeg	Cereals or starch, wild nutmeg.
Pepper	*Refuse of all sorts*, *pepper dust*, *ground crackers*, *or ship stuff*; *rice*, *mustard hulls*, *charcoal*, cocoanut shells, *cayenne*, beans, *bran*, *yellow corn.*
Mustard	*Cereals and starch*, *turmeric*, peas, *yellow corn meal*, *ginger*, *gypsum.*

The materials in italics have been identified in spices examined in the laboratory of this division, but some of the commoner adulterants have not been found. Considering the spices individually, there are certain peculiarities, as they are met with pure and in the trade, which should not be overlooked.

MUSTARD.

Mustard, as sold in the ground state, should be the farina or flour of the black or white mustard seed—that is to say, the flour from the interior of the seed bolted or separated from the hulls. The two kinds of seed, although derived from plants of the same genus, are somewhat different in their chemical composition. The black seed is much the most pungent, and develops, on mixing with water, a volatile oil, which gives this condiment its penetrating character. There is also present in the seed a complicated organic substance of a bitter nature, to which is due some of the peculiar flavor, and while the white seed forms no volatile oil with water, it contains more of the bitter substance. It is, therefore, very common to mix the two in grinding. The sources of the seed are various. In our markets at present there are quoted California black and white, Dutch, Trieste black, and English—the last being the most valuable.

In the manufacture of the seed into flour for the market, two customs have arisen which change the nature of the original substance, and therefore would commonly come under the head of adulteration. One is extremely old, the addition of wheat flour for the purpose of making the condiment keep better. This necessitates the restoration of the yellow color by turmeric, or other dye-stuff. These diluents are harmless as a rule, but there seems to be no reasons for their use, and it is gradually becoming commoner to find mustard free from them in English brands.

The other custom is the abstraction of the fixed oil by pressure before grinding the seed. The percentage of this oil is over 30. It adds nothing to the flavor of the mustard, probably injures its keeping qualities, makes the seed more difficult to mill, and its removal is therefore a benefit. It is a nearly universal custom at the present day in this country, and is not considered as fraudulent by the Canadian analysts.

Falsifications of mustard other than those mentioned are not common, although gypsum has been found in low-grade mustard and several other adulterants, among them ginger of low grade. The hulls bolted from the flour in the process of manufacture are preserved and form the basis of the adulteration of many other spices.

PEPPER, BLACK AND WHITE.

Pepper is more in demand than any other spice, and in consequence is more adulterated. Its appearance in the ground form, especially of the black, is such as to make it possible to use all sorts of refuse for this purpose, and almost everything that has been used as an adulterant has been found in pepper. White pepper, which is simply the black deprived of its outer black coats, is, of course, less easily falsified; but in France is diluted to an immense extent with ground olive stones, which bear a striking resemblance. Among the samples from Washington grocers, pepper sweepings—that is, husks and dirt—rice or corn, and mustard-hulls were the commonest admixtures. Sand is said to be very commonly added abroad, but has not been met with here. In Canada and New York ground cocoanut-shells are a cheap source of adulteration, but they have not extended so far south.

Specimens from Baltimore mills of very low-quality goods were found to contain but little pepper, and that of the worst quality, being made up of cracker dust, yellow corn, cayenne, and charcoal in so disgraceful a way as to be visible to the unassisted eye on close examination.

The quality of a ground pepper can be told by an expert from its weight and color, and on examination with a lens of low magnifying power. The particles are not coarsely ground, and it is not difficult to pick out pieces of husk, yellow corn, and rice, and, if necessary, a more careful investigation under a microscope of higher power will serve for confirmation. Black pepper, in our experience, is much more liable to adulteration than white, although it is perfectly easy to dilute the latter with broken rice or cracker dust, which are inexpensive. All these materials, fortunately, owing to the grossness of the adulteration, are readily recognized, and there is hardly the necessity for recourse to chemical analysis. There has been, however, considerable investigation in this direction, so that there are means of confirming the optical examination which are of great value. Determination of the amount of starch is one of the methods upon which some reliance can be placed; for, if under the microscope foreign starch is not detected, then the addition of "P. D." or other starch free adulterants, will diminish the percentage found, and the reverse. In this way, too, one is able to arrive at an approximate conclusion as to the proportion of adulterants added, which can only be estimated within wide limits under the microscope.

In spite of the immense amount of adulteration, it is possible, from the best shops, to obtain pure ground peppers, but it is at the same time safer with a family spice-mill to grind the whole berries as they are needed. The sources of our pepper supply are Tellicherry on the west coast of Hindostan, which is graded high, and Penang and Singapore for the east, Sumatra, Java, &c. The importations are principally through London, and not direct. The supply of ground pepper from England will usually be found more pure than our own brands, and at the same time is naturally more expensive.

CAYENNE OR RED PEPPER.

This condiment should consist of the ground pods of any of several species of *Capsicum*, known as chilies or peppers. It is said to have been adulterated with many substances, brick dust, red lead, and coloring matters; but this has only been found to be the case in two cheap Baltimore cayennes, while in Washington only rice has been detected, but that quite frequently. Inferior material is no doubt often ground, but the small value of the pods and the small quantity consumed does not tend to increase adulteration.

GINGER.

Ginger is the root, or, technically, rhizome, of a plant somewhat similar in appearance to our iris and flag. It is grown in various parts of the world and prepared with great care and great carelessness, being at times scraped and bleached, at others simply dried in any condition, so that there is an immense number of varieties and qualities to be found in the market. They all, however, retain sufficiently the marked peculiarities of the starchy fibrous root to make the detection of adulterants easy. The common ones are the addition of wheat flour or some starch as a diluent, the coloring with turmeric to suit a popular fancy for gingerbread or of spent material which has been used in making tincture. Mustard hulls and cayenne are also found in some cases, but have seldom been detected here. They are added to give pungency and make up for the addition of flour. Their detection is easy. The sources of our supply are Jamaica and the West Indies, Cochin China, Africa and India. Jamaica is the best and most carefully prepared.

CLOVES.

The flower buds of the clove tree carefully picked and dried constitute the spice known by that name. Their valuable properties are due to the volatile oil which they contain, the best having as much as 16 per cent.

The removal of this oil is so very easy that it is the commonest method of deception to do so before grinding the spice and to then dispose of it as pure. We have ready means of determining the loss chemically, but the microscope gives no indications. The addition of the cheaper clove stems is also practiced, as they cost but 6 cents when the buds cost 27. The microscope reveals their presence by certain cells which they contain which are absent in the buds.

Pimento is sometimes substituted in part or entirely, as it has a clove-like flavor but only 4 or 5 per cent. of volatile oil. It is worth less than one fifth the price of cloves. Its chemical composition and its structure, that of a berry, reveals its presence. The addition of the coarser adulterants, mineral matter, cocoanut shells, flour, peas, and the like, have only been observed in two instances, but no doubt frequently occur, as has been found in Canada.

The sources of our supply are the East Indies (Amboyna), African (Zanzibar), and American, ranking in value in the order named. Cloves should, if possible, be always purchased whole, as they deteriorate less readily in that form.

CINNAMON AND CASSIA.

These spices are the barks of several species of the genus *Cinnamonum*, the true cinnamon being a native of Ceylon, where it is largely cultivated, and the cassias being derived from several other species growing in China, India, and the East Indies. Cinnamon as it reaches the market is very thin, the outer and inner coats of the bark having been removed. Cassia on the other hand is thick, as it consists of the entire bark and can be distinguished by its retaining its natural outer surface. Cinnamon is by far more valuable than the cassia, as there is a smaller supply and intrinsically it contains a much greater proportion of volatile oil and that of higher and more delicate aroma. In consequence cassia is largely substituted for cinnamon, and in fact not a particle of ground cinnamon can be found in the market. It can be found in the whole condition in good quality only in drug stores. Cassia exists in many forms and qualities, and sells at wholesale at from 7 to 40 cents a pound. That known as Saigon is the best, and that exported from Batavia the poorest. Cassia buds also hold a small place in the market.

The detection of the substitution of cassia for cinnamon, since the barks are of trees of the same species, is more difficult than is usually the case and may prove troublesome to a novice. The presence of more woody fiber in the latter with the aid of chemical analysis serves, however, as a reliable distinction. In the samples which have come into our hands not a particle of material labeled ground cinnamon proved to be anything other than cassia. The spice millers appeared, however, to be satisfied to stop at this point and in only one case was there addition of cheap stuff to the cassia. When added there is no difficulty in detecting it as has been done here and in Canada, where peas, starch, ground shells, and crackers have been found in powder labeled both cassia and cinnamon.

The barks can, in most cases, and especially the cinnamon, be used nearly as well in the whole condition and should at least be so purchased and then ground. A slight acquaintance with the appearance of the different qualities will teach one the proper selection to make.

NUTMEG AND MACE.

These spices are different portions of the fruit of a tree known as the nutmeg tree, *Myristica fragrans*, the nutmeg being the inner kernel and the mace one of the outer coats or arillus. The tree grows principally on the Banda Islands and the spices reach us through London. They can always be obtained in their original condition and should be so purchased. When ground they are mixed with diluents of various descriptions, principally cereals and their refuse, wh ch are easily detected.

Owing to the infrequency of the sale of the powdered nutmeg and mace, their adulteration has attracted but little attention.

SOURCES OF OUR SPICE SUPPLY.

Although the countries where the spices are grown have been already given in a general way and in a later chapter will be given more in detail, these countries, in many instances, are not the direct sources of our supplies. For instance, of the pepper imported in the fiscal year ending June 30, 1886, amounting to nearly 12,000,000 pounds, over 8,000,000 came to us from England, and about 3,000,000 from the British East Indies, including the ports of Singapore and Penang. In regard to the other spices data are found in the annual statement of the Bureau of Statistics of the Treasury Department and in some additional tables furnished to this office by the Bureau, which are here given:

Imports of unground spices, free of duty, for the year ending June 30, 1886.

Countries from which imported.	Nutmegs.		Pepper.		All other.	
	Quantity.	Value.	Quantity.	Value.	Quantity.	Value.
	Pounds.		*Pounds.*		*Pounds.*	
Argentine Republic						
Austria			2,128	$223		
Belgium						
Brazil					194	$32
Central American States:						
Costa Rica						
Guatemala			12	1		
Honduras						
Nicaragua						
San Salvador						
Chili			5,905	498		
China	11,825	83,982	344,552	45,808	257,402	21,737
Denmark						
Danish West Indies						
Greenland, Iceland, and the Faroe Islands						
France						
French West Indies	300	120				
French Guiana						
Miquelon, Langley, and Saint Pierre Islands						
French Possessions in Africa and adjacent islands						
French Possessions, all other						
Germany	4,740	2,293			16,831	1,892
England	247,839	96,412	8,214,037	1,157,204	2,097,255	176,505
Scotland						
Ireland						
Gibraltar						
Nova Scotia, New Brunswick, and Prince Edward Island						
Quebec, Ontario, Manitoba, and the Northwest Territory			1,465	338	719	35
British Columbia						
Newfoundland and Labrador						
British West Indies	3,344	889	480	9	3,917,943	146,880
British Guiana						
British Honduras						
British East Indies	464,862	179,169	2,927,472	403,090	1,086,938	66,536
Hong-Kong					1,089,989	91,650
British Possessions in Africa and adjacent islands			11,984	1,942	1,563,073	59,101
British Possessions in Australasia						
British Possessions, all other			840	66		
Greece						
Hawaiian Islands						
Hayti						
Italy						
Japan						
Liberia					4,233	298
Mexico	50	37	48,255	7,328	907	109
Netherlands	219,635	83,412			31,038	7,292
Dutch West Indies						
Dutch Guiana						
Dutch East Indies	245,942	90,065	3,261	390	817,756	35,618
Peru						
Portugal						
Azore, Madeira, and Cape Verde Islands						
Portuguese Possessions in Africa and adjacent islands						
Roumania						
Spain					151	36
Cuba					856	241
Porto Rico					101,338	4,302
Sweden and Norway						
Switzerland						
Turkey in Europe						
Turkey in Asia						
Venezuela					1,160	89
All other countries and ports in Asia						
All other countries and ports in Africa			283,092	28,151	851,307	66,624
Total	1,189,507	458,379	11,843,433	1,644,383	10,767,211	678,936

Imports of ground spices, dutiable, for the year ending June 30, 1886.

Countries from which imported.	Quantity.	Value.
	Pounds.	
Argentine Republic	....	....
Austria	991	$225
Belgium	....	....
Brazil	....	....
Central American States:		
Costa Rica	....	....
Guatemala	....	....
Honduras	....	....
Nicaragua	....	....
San Salvador	....	....
Chili	....	....
China	1	1
Denmark	50	8
Danish West Indies	....	....
Greenland, Iceland, and the Faroe Islands	....	....
France	3, 028	913
French West Indies	....	....
French Guiana	....	....
Miquelon, Langley, and Saint Pierre Island	....	....
French Possessions in Africa and adjacent islands	....	....
French Possessions, all other	....	....
Germany	556	103
England	644, 022	164, 667
Scotland	....	....
Ireland	1, 758	611
Gibraltar	....	....
Nova Scotia, New Brunswick, and Prince Edward Island	5	1
Quebec, Ontario, Manitoba, and the Northwest Territory	115	15
British Columbia	....	....
Newfoundland and Labrador	....	....
British West Indies	....	....
British Guiana	....	....
British Honduras	....	....
British East Indies	....	....
Hong-Kong	114	$8
British Possessions in Africa and adjacent islands	....	....
British Possessions in Australasia	....	....
British Possessions, all other	....	....
Greece	....	....
Hawaiian Islands	....	....
Hayti	....	....
Italy	22	2
Japan	....	....
Liberia	....	....
Mexico	448	72
Netherlands	3, 312	246
Dutch West Indies	....	....
Dutch East Indies	....	....
Peru	....	....
Azores, Madeira, and Cape Verde Islands	....	....
Russia on the Baltic and White Seas	1, 101	93
San Domingo	....	....
Spain	35, 442	3, 087
Cuba	2, 734	351
Porto Rico	....	....
Philippine Islands	....	....
Sweden and Norway	....	....
Switzerland	....	....
Turkey in Europe	....	....
Turkey in Asia	....	....
United States of Colombia	....	....
Uruguay	....	....
Venezuela	....	....
All other countries and ports in Africa	....	....
Total	693, 699	170, 423

Statement showing, by customs districts and ports the quantities and values of spices imported and entered for consumption in the United States during the year ending June 30, 1886.

FREE OF DUTY.

Customs districts and ports.	Cassia buds.		Cassia, cassia vera.		Cinnamon, and chips of	
	Quantity.	Value.	Quantity.	Value.	Quantity.	Value.
	Pounds.		*Pounds.*		*Pounds.*	
Aroostook, Me	....	....	....	....	....	....
Baltimore, Md	....	....	....	....	12, 127	$824. 00
Boston, Mass	....	....	....	....	....	....
Brazos de Santiago, Tex	....	....	....	....	....	....
Chicago, Ill	....	....	....	....	....	....
Cincinnati, Ohio	....	....	....	....	....	....
Corpus Christi, Tex	....	....	....	....	....	....
Detroit, Mich	....	....	....	....	....	....
Duluth, Minn	....	....	....	....	....	....
Galveston, Tex	....	....	....	....	....	....
Key West, Fla	....	....	....	....	2	. 50
Middletown, Conn	....	....	....	....	....	....
Minnesota, Minn	....	....	....	....	....	....
New Orleans, La	....	....	....	....	....	....
New York, N. Y	232, 718	$14, 496	1, 838, 649	114, 681	64, 555	10, 274. 00
Oregon, Oreg	....	....	....	....	....	....
Oswegatchie, N. Y	....	....	....	....	....	....
Paso del Norte, Tex	....	....	....	....	....	....
Philadelphia, Pa	5, 313	566	12, 451	978	....	....
Saluria, Tex	....	....	....	....	....	....
San Francisco, Cal	....	....	....	....	....	....
Saint Louis, Mo	....	....	....	....	2, 243	387. 00
Willamette, Oreg	....	....	....	....	....	....
Total	238, 031	15, 062	1, 851, 100	115, 659	78, 927	11, 485. 50

Statement showing, by customs districts and ports, the quantities and values of spices imported and entered for consumption, &c.—Continued.

FREE OF DUTY.

Customs districts and ports.	Cloves.		Clove stem.		Ginger root.	
	Quantity.	Value.	Quantity.	Value.	Quantity.	Value.
	Pounds.		*Pounds.*		*Pounds.*	
Aroostook, Me						
Baltimore, Md	11,098	$1,500.00			88,214	$4,961.00
Boston, Mass	20,708	2,632.00	30,000	$675.00	954,716	38,664.00
Brazos de Santiago, Tex						
Chicago, Ill	6,606	1,011.00			95	1.00
Cincinnati, Ohio	3,931	601.00				
Corpus Christi, Tex						
Detroit, Mich						
Duluth, Minn	742	35.00				
Galveston, Tex						
Key West, Fla	30	6.20				
Middletown, Conn						
Minnesota, Minn						
New Orleans, La						
New York, N. Y	1,234,576	145,634.00	266,127	5,057.00	3,192,245	174,178.00
Oregon, Oreg					420	4.00
Oswegatchie, N. Y						
Paso del Norte, Tex						
Philadelphia, Pa	13,001	1,732.00			34,534	2,392.00
Saluria, Tex						
San Francisco, Cal						
Saint Louis, Mo	8,101	1,232.00			966	51.00
Willamette, Oreg					5,900	194.00
Total	1,298,683	154,383.20	296,127	5,732.00	4,277,110	220,415.00

FREE OF DUTY.

Customs districts and ports.	Mace.		Nutmegs.		Pepper, white and black.	
	Quantity.	Value.	Quantity.	Value.	Quantity.	Value.
	Pounds.		*Pounds.*		*Pounds.*	
Aroostook, Me						
Baltimore, Md			22,314	$8,634	429,849	$57,075
Boston, Mass	6,733	$1,907.00	66,465	27,462	476,900	54,951
Brazos de Santiago, Tex					460	102
Chicago, Ill					23,746	3,575
Cincinnati, Ohio					139,726	20,424
Corpus Christi, Tex						
Detroit, Mich						
Duluth, Minn						
Galveston, Tex						
Key West, Fla	115	11.50				
Middletown, Conn						
Minnesota, Minn						
New Orleans, La						
New York, N. Y	115,022	28,617.00	1,008,282	395,583	9,119,301	1,309,084
Oregon, Oreg						
Oswegatchie, N. Y					1,465	338
Paso del Norte, Tex						
Philadelphia, Pa	139	118.00	177	162	195,455	25,703
Saluria, Tex					25	8
San Francisco, Cal			86,014	23,643	509,882	71,296
Saint Louis, Mo			6,204	2,858	98,887	15,255
Willamette, Oreg						
Total	122,009	30,653.50	1,189,456	458,342	10,995,786	1,557,810

Statement showing, by customs districts and ports, the quantities and values of spices imported and entered for consumption, &c.—Continued.

FREE OF DUTY.

Customs districts and ports.	Pepper, cayenne.		Pimento.		All other, n. s. e., or p. f.	
	Quantity.	Value.	Quantity.	Value.	Quantity.	Value.
	Pounds.		*Pounds.*		*Pounds.*	
Aroostook, Me						
Baltimore, Md						
Boston, Mass			130	$4	11,585	920.00
Brazos de Santiago, Tex						
Chicago, Ill						
Cincinnati, Ohio						
Corpus Christi, Tex	9,552	$1,296			37,446	6,111.00
Detroit, Mich						
Duluth, Minn						
Galveston, Tex						
Key West, Fla					54	5.20
Middletown, Conn						2,400.00
Minnesota, Minn						
New Orleans, La						
New York, N. Y	723,459	73,789	2,500,523	109,605	33,600	
Oregon, Oreg						
Oswegatchie, N. Y						
Paso del Norte, Tex	1,081	47				
Philadelphia, Pa	79,118	5,503	130	6		
Saluria, Tex						
San Francisco, Cal					151,313	21,511.00
Saint Louis, Mo					16,329	1,265.00
Willamette, Oreg						
Total	813,210	80,635	2,500,783	109,615	250,327	32,212.20

DUTIABLE.

Customs districts and ports.	Mustard, ground or preserved, in bottles, or o.		All other, ground or produced, n. s. e. or p. f.	
	Quantity.	Value.	Quantity.	Value.
	Pounds.		*Pounds.*	
Aroostook, Me	4½	$1.35		
Baltimore, Md	10,660	2,839.00		
Boston, Mass	24,670	7,074.00	894	$392.00
Brazos de Santiago, Tex				
Chicago, Ill				
Cincinnati, Ohio				
Corpus Christi, Tex			6	1.00
Detroit, Mich	896	278.00		
Duluth, Minn	5	1.00	20	5.00
Galveston, Tex	1,800	317.00		349.41
Key West, Fla	3	.42	2,762	246.00
Middletown, Conn			3,312	9.00
Minnesota, Minn			90	3,704.00
New Orleans, La	45,207	8,810.00	36,982	498.00
New York, N. Y	404,099	100,609.00	2,295	
Oregon, Oreg				
Oswegatchie, N. Y				
Paso del Norte, Tex			442	70.62
Philadelphia, Pa	106,735	30,701.00	420	157.00
Saluria, Tex				
San Francisco, Cal	38,985	11,195.00		
Saint Louis, Mo	4,490	1,111.00		
Willamette, Oreg			94½	5.26
Total	637,555½	162,936.77	47,317½	5,431.29

Unfortunately, with the exception of pepper and nutmeg, the tables giving the countries from which the imports were made do not distinguish between the spices. We are, however, able to see that a large portion of our supply comes through England, and the effect of this upon its quality is certainly not to improve it. The amount of each spice entered for consumption is visible in the last table and the port of arrival as well. New York of course receives the largest portion, followed by Boston and Baltimore, which are both milling centers.

As the spices are offered by the wholesale merchant they have a variable value, the quotations in New York for the week ending December 27, 1886, being as follows:

Kind of spices.	Price per pound.		Kind of spices.	Price per pound.	
	Cents.			*Cents.*	
Cassia:			Nutmegs, 110s	48 to 50	
Batavia	7 to	7½	Pepper:		
China		5¾	Singapore		18
Saigon:			West coast	15¾	16
Rolls	36	40	Acheen, prime		15
Broken		30	Penang, white	25	26
Chips	9	10	Singapore, white	28½	29
Buds	10½	10¾	Red:		
Cloves:			Zanzibar	8½	9
Prime		27	Bombay		6
Amboyna		27	Pimento, prime		5
Stems		6	Mustard:		
Ginger:			California:		
African		5	Brown	3½	4¼
Calcutta	3¾	4	Yellow	3¾	4½
Cochin	10	13	Dutch	5¾	6
Mace:			English	6¼	6½
Batavia		50	Trieste, brown	5½	5¾
Banda		50			
Penang		50			

It is of interest to examine these figures and compare them with the prices of wholesalers and retailers of ground spices.

The following figures show that prices alone are often a good indication of adulteration, the ground article being sold at wholesale or even retail for less than the cost of the pure unground spice.

Pure whole spices	Price per pound.		
	Wholesale.		Small lots.
	Cents.		*Cents.*
Ginger root:			
Bleached:			
Jamaica	....		16
American	....		14
Unbleached:			
Jamaica	....		14
Cochin	7½ to 11		12
Calcutta	3¾	4	8
Clove stems		6	10
Clove:			
Singapore	26½	27	30
Amboyna		27	32
Pepper:			
White Singapore		28½	32
Best west coast	15¾	16	18
Acheen		15½	18
Mustard seed:			
Brown Trieste	5½	5¾	12
Yellow English	6¼	6½	12
California	3½	4¼	8
Brown California	3¾	4½	8
Cassia bark:			
Batavia	7	7½	10
Saigon stick	36	40	12
Saigon chip	9	10	10
Ligna sticks	....		9
Singapore black pepper	17¼	17¾	....
Zanzibar red pepper		9½	10

Prices as supplied by spice mills.

Name.	Price per pound.	
	Wholesale, barrels.	Small lots in tin.
	Cents.	*Cents.*
Durham mustard	12	16
Extra strong mustard	16	20
Extra American mustard	18	22
B. Pure Pepper	12	16
Best pepper	10	14
Pure cinnamon	12	16
Best cinnamon	10	14
Pure ginger	7	11
Best ginger	6	10
Pure cayenne	12	16
Best cayenne	10	14
Pure allspice	6	10
Best allspice	5	9
Pure cloves	20	24
Best cloves	17	21
Pure mace	50	54
Pure white pepper	25	29

CHARACTER OF THE SPICES IN THE DISTRICT OF COLUMBIA.

The spices found in Washington are from various markets. The first class grocers carry the best English and rarely good American brands. Adulteration, however, is frequent, especially among the mustards, peppers, and cinnamon, the first having lost its oil and added flour, and the last having cassia substituted for it. Among the cheaper class of dealers adulterated spices are nearly universal, the supply being obtained largely from Baltimore and to a small extent ground in Washington, both places in which yellow corn and charcoal are much used as adulterants.

Of a series of samples collected impartially from all classes of shops the ratio of adulterated to non-adulterated was as follows:

Variety of spice.	Pure.	Adulterated.	Substituted.	Inferior or suspicious.
Cassia	3			1
Cinnamon			10	
Cloves		2		9
Ginger	4	4		
Mace	3	2		
Mustard		10 *		1
Nutmeg	3			
Pepper:				
Black	1	9		
White	2	2		
Red	1	5		
Pimento	5	3		1

* Oil expressed in one case and tumeric added and oil expressed in all American brands.

The preceding samples, which have proved to be so largely adulterated, have been used in connection with a collection of authenticated whole spices obtained directly from the importers as a means of investigating the methods which have been recommended for the detection of adulterants, and the results of our examination of published methods and our own work are presented in the following pages, giving to the analyst a large amount of technical and scientific information which is of less interest to the general reader.

PART II.

THE DETECTION OF ADULTERATION OF SPICES AND CONDIMENTS.

In attempting to detect the adulteration of spices and condiments the methods which can be employed are of three kinds and depend upon the differences in structure between the adulterants and the substances to which they are added, and upon their proximate composition. The former differences are recognized by mechanical separation and the use of the microscope and the latter by chemical analysis. In the use of the microscope a knowledge of and ability to recognize the principal tissues which constitute the particular plant parts which are used as spices and also of those used as adulterants is necessary, while in the chemical examination the principles of proximate analysis must be understood and applied.

It is as necessary that the analyst should be thoroughly acquainted with the application of the microscope to the determination of cellular structure as to be able to make determinations of proximate principles in the substances under examination. In fact, a mechanical separation and microscopical examination is much more expeditious and more at the command of the majority of persons searching for adulteration.

Chemical analysis requires a systematic and extensive investigation of large numbers of samples, both pure and adulterated, to fix a standard of comparison, and this has hitherto been seldom done, owing to the elaborate nature of the work and the expense involved. It should not be neglected, however, since it serves as a most certain confirmation of the microscopic results, besides furnishing information in regard to the quality of the specimen examined and as to the quantity of any adulterant, which cannot be obtained in any other way. While, therefore, the microscopic method will always retain its value for preliminary and qualitative examinations, it must, with the development of the means of chemical investigation, become more and more a mere adjunct of the latter, as in fact the microscope has become in all branches of science. The application of the microscope to the detection of adulterants will, therefore, be considered first.

MECHANICAL SEPARATION AND MICROSCOPIC EXAMINATION OF SPICES AND CONDIMENTS.

As a preliminary to the microscopic examination a mechanical separation by means of sieves of different mesh furnishes a means of detecting adulterants and selecting particles for further investigation, which is of the greatest value and often reveals without additional means the presence of foreign materials. Many adulterants are not ground as fine as the spice to which they are added, and by passing the substance through a sieve of from 40 to 60 meshes to the inch the coarser particles remaining will either be recognized at once by the unaided eye or with a pocket lens or the microscope. In this way turmeric is readily separated from mustard, and yellow corn, mustard hulls and cayenne from low-grade peppers; in no case was the aid of more than an ordinary pocket lens necessary for subsequent recognition, although higher powers of the microscope were confirmatory.

Without entering here into the practical manipulation of the microscope, it may be said that for the purposes of the food analyst it is only necessary to have a stand of good workmanship, not necessarily, though preferably, furnished with substage condenser, but supplied with Nicol prisms for the use of polarized light. Objectives of inch, half-inch, or, for some of the starches, one-fifth inch equivalent focus are sufficient. One eye-piece of medium depth is also enough. It is also desirable to be provided with a dissecting microscope for selecting particles for examination from large masses of ground spice. For those who can afford it, the large stand of Zeiss made for this purpose proves most useful, but simpler forms or even a hand lens will serve perfectly well.

For smaller apparatus it is unnecessary to provide anything aside from what is found in ordinary laboratories. A few beakers, watch glasses, stirring rods, and specimen tubes, with bottles for reagents will be sufficient in addition to the ordinary glass slides and cover glasses.

The reagents which are required include, in case no permanent mounts are required:

Alcohol, strong.
Ammonia.
Chloralhydrat, solution 8 parts to 5 of water.
Glycerine.
Iodine solution: water 15 parts, iodide of potash 20 parts, iodine 5 parts.
Water, distilled.
Schulze's reagent, a mixture of chlorate of potash and dilute nitric acid prepared as wanted.

Balsam in benzol and glycerine jelly are desirable for mounting media and some sheet wax for making cells.

In addition the analyst should supply himself with specimens of whole spices, starches, and known adulterants which can be used to become acquainted with the forms and appearances to be expected. It is easier to begin one's study in this way on sections prepared with the knife than upon the powdered substance, and it is often necessary to refer to them for comparison in the examination of trade samples.

PHYSIOLOGICAL STRUCTURE IN THE SPICES AND THEIR ADULTERANTS.

The vegetable tissues which made up the structure of the spices, and the material of a vegetable origin which are added as adulterants, consist of cells of different forms and thickness. Those which are most prominent and common are the parenchyma, the sclerenchyma, fibrous tissue, and the fibro-vascular bundles. Spiral and dotted vessels are also common in several of the adulterants, and in the epidermis other forms of tissue which it is necessary to be well acquainted with though not physiologically. The parenchyma is the most abundant tissue in all material of vegetable origin, making up the largest proportion of the main part of the plant. It is composed of thin-walled cells, which may be recognized in the potato and in the interior of the stems of maize. In the latter plant, also, the fibro-vascular system is well exemplified, running as scattered bundles between the nodes or joints, and easily made out.

Fibrous tissue consists of elongated thick-walled cells or fibers which are very common in the vegetable kingdom and are well illustrated in flax. They are not as common in spices as in the adulterants. They are optically active, and in the shorter forms somewhat resemble the cells next described. They are seen in one of the coats of buckwheat hulls and in the outer husk of the cocoanut.

The sclerenchyma is found in the shells of many nuts and in one or two of the spices. The cells are known as stone cells, from the great thickening of their walls, and to them is due the hardness of the shell of the cocoanut, the pits of the olive, &c. Their structure is illustrated in Fig. 5 from Strasburger.

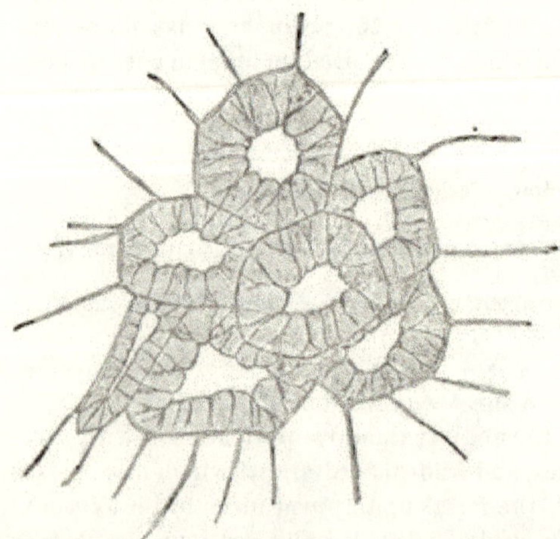

FIG. 5. Sclerenchyma or stone cells. × 210. (After Strasburger.)

Spiral and dotted vessels are common in woody tissue and are readily recognized. With all these forms the analyst should familiarize himself, and as an aid may consult Bessey's Botany in the American Science Series.

In pepper and in mustard the parenchyma cells are prominent in the interior portion of the berry, while those constituting the outer coats are indistinct from their deep color in the pepper, but in the mustard characteristic of the particular species. In fact, in many of the spices, especially those which are seeds, the forms of the epidermal cells are very striking, and even if no attempt is made to classify them their peculiarities must be carefully noted, as the recognition of the presence of foreign husky matter depends upon a knowledge of the normal appearance in any spice. The fibro-vascular bundles are most prominent in ginger and in the barks, where in the powdered spices they are found as stringy particles.

The sclerenchyma or stone cells, are commoner in the adulterants, especially in cocoanut shells, where may also be seen numerous spiral cells and in the exterior coats fibrous tissue.

As aids to distinguishing these structures, the following peculiarities may be cited.

The stone cells and fibrous tissue are optically active and are therefore readily detected with polarized light, shining out in the dark field of the microscope as silver white or yellowish bodies.

The fibro-vascular bundles are stained deep orange brown with iodine, owing to the nitrogenous matter which they contain, while parenchyma is not affected by this reagent aside from the cell contents, nor has it any action on polarized light, remaining quite invisible in the field with crossed prisms.

STARCH.

Aside from the cellular tissue, starch is the most important element in the plant for the analyst, and its peculiarities will be considered quite fully.

It possesses an organized structure and is distinguished by its reaction with iodine solution, with which it strikes a deep blue or blackish blue color, varying somewhat with different kinds of starch and with the strength of the reagent.

Conversely its absence is marked by no blue color under the same circumstances. Heat, however, as in the process of baking, so alters starches, converting them into dextrine and related bodies, that they give a brown color with iodine instead of a blue black. They are then in fact no longer starch, although their form, often not being essentially changed, permits of their identification.

Although a practical experience in recognizing the starches by these characteristics is essential for their rapid detection when occurring as adulterants, a valuable guide may be supplied to a certain extent by artificial classifications, such as Vogel, Muter, and Blyth, after Tripe's work, have arranged.

Vogel's and Muter's are based on the form and size ot the granules, of the hilum or central depression or nucleus and the prominence and position of the rings. Tripe showed that with polarized light and selenite the starches of tubers showed a more varied play of colors than the cereal and leguminous starches which are produced above ground. On this fact Blyth has made another classification. Both are of value and interest.

Vogel's table of the different starches and arrowroots of commerce.

A.—Granules simple, bounded by rounded surfaces.

I. Nucleus central, layers concentric.
- *a.* Mostly round or from the side lens-shaped.
  1. Large granules .0396 – .0528^{mm}, *rye starch.*
  2. Large granules .0352 – .0396^{mm}, *wheat starch.*
  3. Large granules .0264, *barley starch.*
- *b.* Egg-shaped, oval, kidney-shaped. Hilum often long and ragged.
  1. Large granules .032 – .079^{mm}, *leguminous starches.*

II. Nucleus eccentric, layers plainly eccentric or meniscus shaped.
- *a.* Granules not at all or only slightly flattened.
  1. Nucleus mostly at the smaller end .06 – .10^{mm}, *potato starch.*
  2. Nucleus mostly at the broader end or towards the middle in simple granules .022 – .060^{mm}, *maranta starch.*
- *b.* Granules more or less strongly flattened.
  1. Many drawn out to a short point at one end.
     - *a.* At most .060^{mm} long, *curcuma starch.*
     - *b.* As much as .132^{mm} long, *canna starch.*
  2. Many lengthened to bean-shaped, disk-shaped, or flattened; nucleus near the broader end .044 – .075^{mm}, *banana starch.*
  3. Many strongly kidney-shaped: nucleus near the edge .042 – .056^{mm}, *sisyrinchium starch.*
  4. Egg-shaped; at one end reduced to a wedge, at the other enlarged; nucleus at smaller end .05 – .07^{mm}, *yam starch.*

B.—Granules simple or compound, single granules or parts of granules, either bounded entirely by plane surfaces, many angled, or by partly round surfaces.

I. Granules entirely angular.
1. Many with prominent nucleus. At most .0066^{mm}, *rice starch.*
2. Without a nucleus. The largest .0088^{mm}, *millet starch.*

II. Among the many angled also rounded forms.
- *a.* No partly rounded forms present, angular form predominating.
  1. Without nucleus or depression very small, .0044^{mm}, *oat starch.*
  2. With nucleus or depression .0132 – .0220^{mm}.
     - *a.* Nucleus or its depression considerably rounded; here and there the granules united into differently formed groups, *buckwheat starch.*
     - *b.* Nucleus mostly radiatory or star-shaped; all the granules free, *maize (corn) starch.*
- *b.* More or less numerous kettle-drum and sugar-loaf like forms.
  1. Very numerous eccentric layers; the largest granules .022 – .0352^{mm}, *batata starch.*
  2. Without layers or rings .08 – .022^{mm}.
     - *a.* In the kettle drum-shaped granules the nucleal depression mostly widened on the flattened side, .008 – .022^{mm}, *cassava starch.*
     - *b.* Depression wanting or not enlarged.
       - *aa.* Nucleus small, eccentric, .008 – .016^{mm}, *pachyrhizus starch.*
       - *bb.* Nucleus small, central, or wanting.
         - *aaa.* Many irregular angular forms .008 – .0176^{mm}, *sechium starch.*
         - *bbb.* But few angular forms; some with radiatory nucleal fissure, .008 – .0176, *castanospermum starch.*

C.—Granules simple and compounds, predominant forms, egg form and oval, with eccentric nucleus and numerous layers, the compound granule made up of a large granule and one or more relatively small kettledrum-shaped ones, .025 – .060^{mm}, *sago starch.*

*Muter's table for the detection of starches when magnified about 230 diameters.**

[All measurements are given in decimals of an inch.]

Group I: All more or less oval in shape and having both *hilum* and rings visible.

Name.	Shape.	Normal measurements.	Remarks.
Tous les mois	Oval, with flat ends	.00370 to .00185	Hilum annular, near one end and incomplete rings.
Potato	Oval	.00270 .00148	Hilum annular, rings incomplete, shape and size very variable.
Bermuda arrowroot	Sack-shaped	.00148 .00129	Hilum distinct annular, shape variable, rings faint.
St. Vincent arrowroot	Oval-oblong	.00148 .00129	Hilum semilunar, rings faint, shape not very variable.
Natal arrowroot	Broadly ovate	.00148 .00129	Hilum annular, in center and well marked complete rings.
Galangal	Skittle-shaped	†.00135	Hilum elongated, very faint incomplete rings.
Calumba	Broadly pear-shaped	†.00185	Hilum semilunar, faint but complete rings, shape variable.
Orris root	Elongated-oblong	†.00092	Hilum faint, shape characteristic.
Turmeric	Oval-oblong, conical	†.00148	Very strongly-marked incomplete rings.
Ginger	Shortly conical, with rounded angles.	†.00148	Hilum and rings scarcely visible, shape variable but characteristic.

Group II: With strongly-developed *hilum* more or less stellate.

Name.	Shape.	Normal measurements.	Remarks.
Bean	Oval-oblong	†.00135	Fairly uniform.
Pea	Like bean	.00111 — .00074	Very variable in size, with granules under .00111 preponderating.
Lentil	Like bean	†.00111	Hilum, a long depression seldom radiate.
Nutmeg	Rounded	†.00055	The small size and rounded form distinctive.
Dari	Elongated hexagon	†.00074	Irregular appearance and great convexity distinctive.
Maize	Round and polygonal	†.00074	The rounded angles of the polygonal granules distinctive.

Group III: Hilum and rings practically invisible.

Name.	Shape.	Normal measurements.	Remarks.
Wheat	Circular and flat	.00185 to .00009	*Very variable* in size and *very dull* polarization in water.
Barley	*Slightly* angular circles	‡.00073	The majority measuring about .00073 distinctive.
Rye	Like barley	.00148 .00009	Small granules, quite round, and here and there cracked.
Jalap	Like wheat		Polarizes *brightly* in water.
Rhubarb	do	.00055 §.00023	Polarizes between jalap and wheat, and runs smaller and more convex.
Senega	do	.00148 — .00009	Measurements the only guide.
Bay berry	do	.00074 — .00011	
Sumbul	do	.00074 — .00009	

*Analyst **1**, 172–174, November 15, 1876.
†About.
‡ And a few four times this size.
§ For small granules.

Muter's table for the detection of starches, &c.—**Continued.**

Group III: **Hilum and rings practically invisible—Continued.**

Name.	Shape.	Normal measurement.	Remarks.
Chestnut	Very variable	.00090 — .00009	Variable form, and small but regular size, distinctive.
Acorn	Round-oval	*.00074	Small and uniform size, distinctive.
Calabar bean	Oval-oblong	.00296 .00160	Large size and shape characteristic.
Liquorice	Elongated-oval	*.00018	Small size and shape distinctive.
Hellebore (green or black)	Perfectly rotund	.00037 .00009	Small, regular size and rotundity, distinctive.
Hellebore (white)	Irregular	.00055 .00009	Irregular shape and faint central depression, distinctive.

Group IV: **More or less truncated at one end.**

Name.	Shape.	Normal measurement.	Remarks.
Cassia	Round	.00111 to .00018	Round or muller shaped granules and faint circular hilum.
Cinnamon	Like cassia	.00074 .00069	More frequently truncated than cassia, and smaller.
Sago (raw)	Oval-ovate	.00260 .00111	Has circular hilum at convex end and rings faintly visible.
Sago (prepared)	do	.00260 .00111	Has a large oval or circular depression, covering one-third nearly of each granule.
Tapioca	Roundish	.00071 .00035	A little over 50 per cent. truncated by one facet, and a pearly *hilum*.
Arum	Like tapioca	*.00056	Smaller than tapioca and truncated by *two* facets.
Belladonna	do		Not distinguishable from tapioca.
Colchicum	do	*.00074	Larger than tapioca and contains many more truncated granules.
Scammony	do	*.00045	Smaller than tapioca, more irregular, and *hilum* not visible.
Canella	Very variable	.00037 — .00022	Very variable, form and small size the only points.
Podophyllum	Like tapioca	*.00040	Like scammony, but has visible *hilum* in most of the granules.
Aconite	do	*.00037	Like tapioca, but half the size.

Group V: **All granules more or less polygonal.**

Name.	Shape.	Normal measurement.	Remarks.
Tacca	Poly or hexagonal	.00075 to .00037	Distinguished from maize by its *sharp* angles.
Oat	Polygonal	*.00037	Larger than rice and hilum visible in some granules.
Rice	do	.00030 — .00020	Measurement using one-eighth or one-twelfth inch power, and then hilum visible.
Pepper	do	.00020 — .00002	Do.
Ipecacuanha	do	*.00018	Some round and truncated granules, adhering in groups of three.

*About.

DIVISION I.—Starches showing a play of colors with polarized light and selenite plate.

Class I. The hilum and concentric rings clearly visible, all the starches oval or ovate, including tous les mois, potato, arrowroot, calumba, orris root, ginger, galangal, and turmeric.

DIVISION II.—Starches showing no iridescence, or scarcely any, when examined by polarized light and selenite.

Class II. The concentric rings all but invisible, hilum stellate, including bean, pea, maize, lentil, dari, and nutmeg.

Class III. Starches having both the concentric rings and hilum invisible in the majority of granules. This important class includes wheat, barley, rye, chestnut, acorn, and many starches in medicinal plants.

Class IV. All the granules truncated at one end. This class includes sago, tapioca and arum, several drugs, and cinnamon and cassia.

Class V. In this class all the granules are angular in form and it includes oats, tacca, rice, pepper, as well as ipecacuanha starch.

Of the starches which are included in the preceding classification but a limited number will be met with in spices and their adulterants or in the commoner foods. One must, however, be able to readily recognize the following:

Starches natural to spices and condiments.	Starches of admixture.
Ginger.	Wheat and other cereals.
Pepper.	Corn.
Nutmeg.	Oats.
Cassia.	Barley.
Pimento.	Potato.
Cinnamon.	Maranta and other arrowroots.
Cayenne.	Rice.
	Bean.
	Pea.
	Sago.
	Buckwheat.

The remainder may be found in other foods and in drugs and cannot well be omitted therefore from our classifications.

No one of these is complete in itself, but from the characters given and with the aid of our illustrations the starches which commonly occur in the substances which are here considered may usually be identified without difficulty.

In practice the manipulation of the microscope and the preparation of the object requires some little experience, but not more than analysts usually have had. For the benefit of those who have had none, it may be said that a small portion of the starch or spice is taken up upon a clean camel's hair brush and dusted upon a common slide. The excess is blown away and what remains moistened with a drop of a mixture of equal parts of glycerine and water or glycerine and camphor-water and covered with a cover glass. It is well to have a small supply of the common starches in a series of tubes, which can be mounted at any moment and used for comparison. They can be permanently mounted by making with cork borers of two sizes a wax cell-ring equal to the diameter of the cover glass, and after cementing the cell to the slide with copal varnish thinned with turpentine and introducing the starch and glycerine mixture, fixing the cover glass on after running some of the cement over the top of the ring. A little experience will enable one to put the right amount of liquid in the cell and to make a preparation which will keep for some time. After several months, however, it is difficult to distinguish the rings which mark the development of the granule, and although for reference as to size and form the preparation is satisfactory, it is always advisable in doubtful cases to examine some fresh material.

For other purposes the starches should be mounted in prepared Canada balsam or dammar by well-known methods. In this medium they can be preserved indefinitely, but are scarcely visible with ordinary illumination, and must be viewed by polarized light, which brings out distinctive characters, not seen as well or at all in other mounts.

Appearance in glycerine and water.—When mounted in the manner already described, or in water alone if for only temporary use, and examined under a microscope with an objective of equivalent focus of one-half to one-fifth inch, and with means for oblique illumination, the starches will display the characteristics which have been mentioned, and which are illustrated on Plates 26, 27, and 28. These illustrations have been drawn from nature by Dr. George Marx, and represent the starches as nearly as possible, as they are seen, and not as in many of the absurd illustrations of the handbooks of microscopists of the past and present day, which are entirely ideal, representing the granules not as extremely translucent bodies, but with the rings or layers as strongly-marked lines. Examined in this manner the size, shape, presence or absence of a nucleus or hilum, and of the rings and their arrangement, can be made out, and the starch referred to its proper position.

Appearance in balsam with polarized light.—Mounted in balsam the starches are scarcely visible under any form of illumination with ordinary light, the index of refraction of the granules and the balsam being so nearly alike. When, however, polarized light is used the effect is a striking one, and is illustrated in Plates 19 to 21. It is very easy to distinguish all the characteristics, except the rings, the center of the cross being at the nucleus of the granule.

With the selenite plate a play of colors is produced, which is peculiar to some of the starches and forms the basis of Blyth's classification.

The principal starches which are met with may be described as follows, in connection with our illustrations, beginning with those of the arrowroot class, including the potato, ginger, and turmeric.

Potato starch.—The starch grains of the potato are very variable in size, being found from .05 to .10^{mm} in length, and in shape from oval and allied forms to irregular and even round in the smallest. These variations are illustrated in Fig. 57, but the frequency of the smaller granules is not as evident as in Figs. 30 and 31. The layers are visible in some granules with great distinctness and in others hardly at all, being rather more prominent in the starch as obtained from a freshly cut surface. The rings are more distinct, too, near the hilum or nucleus, which in this, as in all tuberous starches, is eccentric, shading off toward the broader or more expanded portion of the granule. The hilum appears as a shadowy depression (Fig. 57) and with polarized light its position is well marked by the junction of the arms of the cross, and it will be found by comparison of Figs. 31 and 32, on Plate XVI, that in the potato it is oftener at the smaller end of the granule and in the arrowroot at the larger. With polarized light and a selenite plate the beautiful play of colors is obtained which is the basis of Blyth's classification. The smaller granules, which are nearly round, may readily be confused with other starches, but their presence serves at once to distinguish this from *Maranta* or *Bermuda arrowroot* starch.

Rarely compound granules are found composed of two or three single ones each with its own nuclus.

Of the same type as the potato starch are the various arrowroots, the only one of which commonly met with in this country being the Bermuda, the starch of the rhizome of *Maranta arundinacea*, and the starch of Turmeric.

Maranta starch.—The granules are usually not so varied in size or shape as those of the potato, as may be seen in Figs. 30, 31, and 32, averaging about .07^{mm} in length. They are about the same size as the average of the latter, but are never found as large or as small, which, together with the fact that the end at which the nucleus appears is broader in the Maranta and more pointed in the potato, enables one to distinguish the starches without difficulty. With polarized light the results are similar to those seen with potato starch, and this is a ready means of distinguishing the two varieties, by displaying in a striking way the form of the granule and position of the hilum, as is illustrated in Figs. 31 and 32.

Curcuma or turmeric starch.—Tumeric contains a starch (Fig. 63, Plate XXVIII), which, although of the arrowroot class, is quite distinct in appearance from those which we have described. It is most irregular in outline, so that it is impossible to define its shape or to do more than refer to the illustration. Many of the granules are long and narrow and drawn out to quite a point. The rings are distinct in the larger ones. The size is about that of the Maranta.

Ginger starch (Figs. 41 and 42, Plate XXI, and Fig. 58, Plate XXVII).—This starch is of the same class as those from the potato and Maranta and several others which are of under-ground origin. In outline it is not oval like those named, but more rectangular, having more obtuse angles in the larger granules and being cylindrical or circular in outline in the smaller.

It averages nearly the same size as Maranta starch, but is much more variable both in size and form. The rings are scarcely visible even with the most favorable illumination.

Sago starch.—This exists in two modifications in the market; as raw and as prepared sago. In the prepared condition it is characterized by a larger circular depression in the center of most of the granules. The rings are not visible. They are mostly circular in form or approaching it, and vary from .025 to .065^{mm} in diameter.

Leguminous starches, pea and bean (Figs. 39 and 40, Plate XX, and Figs. 60 and 61, Plate XXVII).—These starches produce but a slight effect with polarized light. The rings are scarcely visible, and the hilum is stellate or much cracked along a median line; the bean more so than the pea, the latter resembling fresh dough kneaded again into the center as in making rolls, and the former the shape assumed by the same after baking. They are both somewhat variable in size, ranging from .025 to .10^{mm} in length.

Nutmeg starch (Fig. 64, Plate XXVIII).—This starch, which in some respects resembles the preceding—the rings being scarcely visible and not iridescent with polarized light—is much smaller in size and quite variable. The larger granules are at times as long at .05^{mm} and the smallest smaller than .005^{mm}. They are of extremely irregular form, with angular depressions and angular outlines, and are distinguished by a budded appearance, caused by the adherence of small granules to the larger.

Capsicum starch (Fig. 67, Plate XXVIII) is nearly circular or rounded, polyhedral in form, with scarcely visible rings, and in most cases a depressed hilum resembling in size and shape corn starch, but having peculiar irregularities, which distinguish it, such as a rosette-like formation on a flattened granule or a round depression at one end. It does not polarize as actively as maize starch, and can be distinguished from rice by the greater angularity of the latter.

Pepper starch (Fig. 65, Plate XXVIII) is the most minute starch that is usually met with, not averaging over .001^{mm}, nor exceeding .005. It is irregularly polyhedral, polarizes well, but requires a high power to discover any detail when a hilum is found. It cannot be confused with other starches.

Cinnamon starch (Fig. 46, Plate XXIV, and Fig. 66, Plate XXVIII) has an extremely irregular, polyhedral or distorted granule, often united in groups with smaller granules adherent to the larger ones. In size it varies from .001 to .025, averaging nearly the latter size. In some granules a hilum can be distinguished, but no rings. It is readily detected with polarized light.

Buckwheat starch (Fig. 62, Plate XXVIII) is very characteristic. It consists of chains or groups of angular granules, with a not very evident circular nucleus and without rings. The outline is strikingly angular and the size not very variable, being about .01 to .015.

Maize or corn starch (Fig. 33, Plate XVII, and Fig. 51, Plate XXVI). —The granules of corn-starch are largely of the same size, from .02 to .03^{mm} in diameter, with now and then a few which are much smaller. They are mostly circular in shape or rather polyhedral, with rounded angles. They form very brilliant objects with polarized light, but with ordinary illumination show but the faintest sign of rings, and a well-developed hilum, at times star-shaped, and at others more like a circular depression.

Rice starch (Figs. 35 and 36, Plate XVIII, and Fig. 55, Plate XXVI) is very similar to corn starch, and easily confused with it, being about the same size. It is, however, distinguished from it by its polygonal form, and its well-defined angles. The hilum is more prominent and more often stellate or linear. Several granules are at times united.

Wheat starch (Fig. 34, Plate XVII, and Fig. 50, Plate XXVI) is quite variable in size, varying from .05 to $.012^{mm}$ in diameter. It belongs to the same class as barley and rye, the hilum being invisible and the rings not prominent. The granules are circular disks in form, and there are now and then contorted depressions resembling those in pea starch. It is the least regular of the three starches named and does not polarize actively.

Barley starch (Fig. 37, Plate XIX, and Fig. 51, Plate XXVI) is quite similar to that of wheat, but does not vary so much in size, averaging $.05^{mm}$; has rings which are much more distinct, and very small granules adhering to the largest in bud-like forms.

Rye starch (Fig. 52, Plate XXVI) is more variable in size, many of the granules not exceeding $.02^{mm}$, while the largest reach .06 to $.07^{mm}$. It lacks distinctive characteristics entirely, and is the most simple in form of all the starches we have described.

Oat starch (Fig. 38, Plate XIX, and Fig. 53, Plate XXVI) is unique, being composed of large compound masses of polyhedral granules from .12 to $.02^{mm}$ in length, the single granules averaging .02 to .015 mm. It does not polarize actively as may be seen in figure and plate, and displays neither rings nor hilum. The illustration shows its nature with accuracy.

Our descriptions, it will be seen, do not agree entirely with those of other authors, which in the same way do not agree among themselves.

This shows a variation in the peculiarities of size, shape, &c., which must be carefully allowed for, and the necessity for every investigator to compare a starch which he is desirous of identifying with authentic specimens.

STRUCTURE AND PECULIARITIES OF THE COMMONER ADULTERANTS.

Before proceeding to the consideration of the normal structure and composition of the spices and condiments and the adulterations detected in commercial specimens, it is well to become familiar with the characteristics of the common adulterants and materials which are liable to be used for this purpose.

The starches have been already described and their value as a means of identifying different vegetable materials noted. By this means we are able to detect the different cereals which are often added as diluents.

Maize, or corn as it is commonly known, is a common adulterant. By selecting particles from the ground material and crushing them the character of the starch may be recognized, but in a cursory examination the first sign of the presence of this cereal is the discovery of one of the thin outer coats of the grain which becomes detached in milling and, being tough, is not readily reduced. In yellow corn it has a peculiar pinkish color and simple structure of longitudinal cells. One should learn to recognize it from a specimen ground for the purpose.

Rice, which in its broken unmarketable form is sometimes used as a diluent, may be recognized by the brilliant appearance of the hard white particles which must be picked out of the spice under a hand lens, crushed, and examined as usual. Rice bran has not been met with.

The two cereals named are the only ones which are commonly met with which introduce starch. Rarely clean *wheat bran* is added, which can be recognized by its distinctive structural character, illustrated in many hand-books, but which can be learned much better from an authentic specimen, which should be soaked in chloral hydrate.

As modified cereals, we find refuse bread, cracker-dust, and ship-bread in which the wheat starch is much changed from its original form by the heat and moisture of the cooking process so that at times it might be confused with a leguminous starch. The softness of the particles and the ease with which they fall to pieces in water reveals the nature of the material. It is a common diluent.

Oil-seed, oil-cake, and husks are very commonly used in many parts of the country for purposes of sophistication. They are most readily recognized by the peculiar structure of the outer coats of the seed. The particles which can usually be found and selected with a dissecting microscope should be examined in alcohol or glycerine, or a mixture of the two, as the outer coats of some seeds, such as mustard, are swollen by water and become indistinct. The appearance of mustard hulls is given on page 172, and the many varieties of the cruciferous seeds resemble it much, so that it is difficult to distinguish them, which is, however, not important. They are generally distinguished by the outer layer of hexagonal cells, and a middle and an inner coating which consist of peculiar angular cells, the latter much larger than the former, which are the most characteristic, and should be compared with specimens of seed of known origin. The structure of some of them is diagramatically presented in fig. 6, from Schimper. After soaking in chloral hydrate the remaining interior layers are perhaps more easily made out, and in some cases after moderate bleaching with nitric acid and chlorate. The interior of these seeds is not blued by iodine.

Peanut or groundnut cake is recognized by the characteristic structure of the red-brown coat which surrounds the seed, which consists of polygonal cells with peculiar saw-toothed thickening of the walls. The seed itself consists of polygonal cells, full of oil and starch granules, which are globular in form and not easily confused with pepper starch.

The structure of the brown membrane is best made out in chloral hydrate, which removes the red color and leaves the fragments of a bright yellow.

Linseed cake distinguished by the fact that its husk is made up of one or two characteristic elements. The outer coat or epiderimis is colorless and swells up in water, forming a mucilage like the mustard seed. Beneath this is a layer of thin round yellow cells, while the third is very characteristic, and consists of narrow, very thick-walled dotted vessels. Next to these is an inner layer of compact polygonal cells, with fairly thin but still thickly dotted white walls and dark-brown contents, containing tannin. The endosperm and embryo are free from starch; nor are they colored yellow by potash, as is the case with mustard and rape cake.

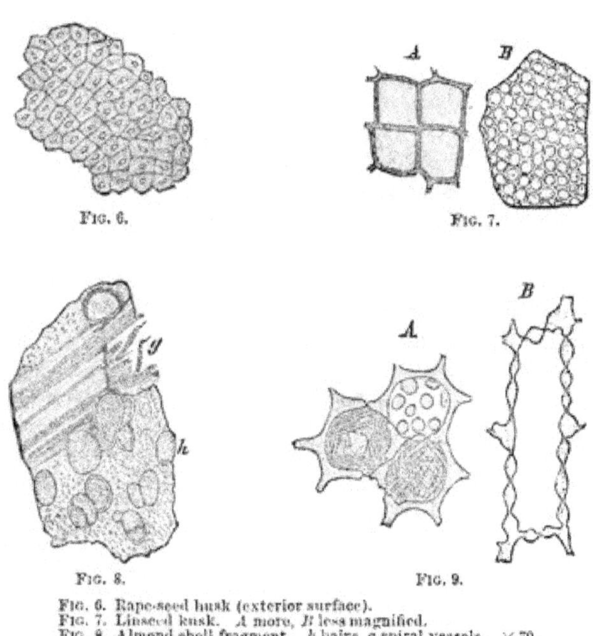

FIG. 6. FIG. 7.

FIG. 8. FIG. 9.

FIG. 6. Rape-seed husk (exterior surface).
FIG. 7. Linseed husk. *A* more, *B* less magnified.
FIG. 8. Almond shell fragment. *h* hairs, *g* spiral vessels. × 70.
FIG. 9. Palm-seed. Interior. × 240. (After Schimper.)

Palm-cake is probably not common enough in this country to be used as an adulterant; nor are *olive stones*, which as they consist, after bleaching with Schulze's reagent, almost entirely of very thick stone cells, are easily made out under polarized light.

Cocoanut shells are often used, it seems from the evidence of the Canadian analysts. They are similar to the olive stones in structure but more complicated, as in addition to the numerous short stone cells there are many long ones with thinner walls, and here and there spiral vessels, from the fibrous tissue, all of which are only readily seen after bleaching. When the shells are roasted or charred they refuse to bleach, and it is then only possible to class the particles on which the reagents do not act as roasted shells or charcoal. They are frequently used in peppers to give color to material rendered too light by white adulterants.

The composition of these substances is shown in the following determination which reveal the effect of their addition upon the normal composition of the spices:

	Olive stones.	Cocoanut shells.
Water	5.63	6.15
Ash	4.28	2.13
Fiber	41.33	37.15
Albuminoids	1.56	1.25
Nitrogen	.25	.20

More in regard to olive stones will be learned when the discussion of the adulteration of pepper is considered.

Buckwheat hulls after bleaching with Schulze's reagent show a preponderance of tissue made up of long, slender, and pointed sclerenchyma cells and a smaller amount of reticulated tissue resembling the cereals somewhat and cayenne pepper. Portions of the endosperm or interior of the seed are also visible, and consist of an agglomeration of small hexagonal cells which originally contained starch. The starch is readily recognized by its peculiar characteristics. The sclerenchyma is, of course, optically active and forms a beautiful and distinctive object with polarized light.

Sawdust of various woods may be recognized by the fragments of various spiral and dotted vessels and fibrous material which are not found in the spices or other adulterants.

Bark, in some parts of the world a common addition to pepper, is detected by its stone cells, which are larger than those of pepper, and of different form and more numerous, and by its fibrous vessels which are made out readily after bleaching. The source of a particular bark cannot, however, be made out.

Rice bran.—This, as several other similar products, is made up prominently of two series of cells at right angles to each other, which make up the outer coats of the grain. The structure is best made out after soaking in chloral-hydrate. The cells of one series are long, small, and thin-walled, and are arranged in parallel bundles. The others have very much thickened walls, and are only two or three times as long as broad. They are at times distinguished, for convenience, as the longitudinal and transverse cells. The remaining layers of the bran are not prominent.

Clove stems, used frequently as a diluent, can be distinguished by their peculiar yellow-dotted vessels and their large and quite numerous stone-cells, neither of which are seen prominently in the substances which are adulterated.

These suggestions of the peculiarites of the different adulterants should, of course, be confirmed and supplemented, and the eye accustomed to recognize their structure by means of a study of the actual substances, which should always be at hand in the dry and ground condition for reference. Quickness and certainty will be much advanced by such facilities.

Reference may also be fittingly made here to chemical operations of a general nature, which are applicable to all the spices.

CHEMICAL EXAMINATION.

Determinations of a quantitative nature should include—

Water.—A portion of the powdered spice which should pass a 60-mesh sieve, one gram, is to be dried at 105° to 110° C. in an air bath, provided with a regulator, until on successive weighings a gain is found showing that oxidation has begun. Twelve hours, or overnight, usually suffices. The loss is water, together with the largest part of the volatile oil. Deduction of the volatile oil, as determined in the ether extract, will give a close approximation to the water.

Ash.—In the same portion the ash is determined by incineration at a very low temperature, such as may be best obtained in a gas muffle, which is a most convenient arrangement for work of this description, and far superior to any kind of lamp or burner. The proportion of ash insoluble in acid may also be determined where there is reason to believe that *sand is present.*

Volatile oil and ether extract.—Two grams of the substance are extracted for twenty hours in a siphoning extraction apparatus on the Soxhlet principle, with Squibbs's best ether. The apparatus we use in this laboratory, arranged by Mr. A. E. Knorr, he describes as follows:

The substance under examination is placed in a test tube, which is then inserted into a continuous extraction apparatus of the intermittent siphon class. The tubes used for this purpose are ordinary test tubes, the bottom of which has been blown out. A wad of washed cotton of sufficient thickness is put into the lower end of the tubes to prevent any solid particles of the sample from finding their way into the receiving flask; another wad of cotton is packed on top of the sample, and the apparatus is then so adjusted that the condensed ether drops into the tube, and, percolating through the sample, siphons into the receiving flask, when the operation is continued *ad infinitum.*

It is absolutely necessary to use the best Squibbs's ether in order to avoid extracting substances other than oil and soluble in alcohol, and to continue the extraction for at least the time named, as piperine and several other proximate principles are not extremely soluble in ether. If these precautions are followed we have found no difficulty in extracting all the piperine, for example, and obtaining duplicate results of great accuracy. On stopping the extraction the extract is washed into a light weighed glass dish, and the ether allowed to evaporate spontaneously and not too rapidly, as in the latter case water is condensed in the dish, which it is difficult to remove. When the ether has disappeared—which ought not to take too long, as in that case some oil is volatilized—the dish is placed in a large dessicator, with pumice and sulphuric acid—chloride of calcium having been shown to be useless*—and allowed to remain overnight, to remove any moisture. The loss of oil by this process is hardly appreciable. The dish is then weighed, and afterwards heated to 110° C. for some hours, to drive off the volatile oil, beginning at a rather low temperature, as the oil is easily oxidized, and then is not volatile. The residue is weighed, the difference being calculated to volatile oil, and then examined as to its composition of purity. The results are fairly satisfactory, as appears from the following duplicates:

Duplicate fat and volatile oil determinations in spices.

No.	Per cent.	Per cent.	No.	Per cent.	Per cent.
4629.....	5.49	8.38	4632.....	4.11	3.66
4629.....	5.23	8.51	4632.....	3.93	4.22
4630.....	5.15	6.54	4633.....	5.06	6.94
4630.....	4.72	6.50	4633.....	5.93	7.68
4631.....	6.64	13.19	4634.....	5.15	3.50
4631.....	6.84	12.14	4634.....	2.26	3.59

Alcohol extract.—This may be made in the same manner as the ether extract, using, of course, the substance already extracted. The solvent may be either absolute alcohol, that of 95 per cent. by volume, or 80 per cent. by weight. The latter is preferable in most cases, as there is no definite point with the stronger spirit at which the extraction is complete.

In the investigation of spices merely for adulteration this extraction is of little value.

Starch, &c., reducing sugars.—The amount of reducing material produced by boiling the spices with dilute acid serves with several as an index of purity. In the case of pepper, which contains naturally a large amount of starch, the addition of the common fibrous adulterants reduces the equivalent of reducing sugars which are indicated by Fehling's solution after boiling with acid. Lenz and several others have examined the value of this determination. The conclusions which are deducible from their experience and our own are that with attention to proper condition to insure complete conversion to dextrose the results are of value, though apt to fall out too low. It has been found desirable in our laboratory to run as a check a parallel determination on a substance of known reduction equivalent. In this way any variation may be detected.

* Fleischer, E., 1884, Zeit. Anal. Chem., 23, 33.

The method of Lenz is described under pepper and its composition. The conditions which we have found most desirable are as follows:

The 2 to 5 grams of the material, usually 4, which should pass an 80-mesh sieve, must be extracted with strong alcohol and with cold water for some time to remove substances not starch which might be acted on by the acid or reduce Fehling's solution. Then, without drying, it is washed off the filter into an Erlenmeyer flask with about 175 c. c. of water and enough strong C. P. hydrochloric acid added, about 25 c. c., to make the liquid 4 to 5 per cent. of acid gas. The flask is then supplied with a condenser and boiled for four hours, or the liquid may be put in a patent rubber-stoppered beer bottle and digested in a steam bath; but the latter method is not as certain. After the boiling and cooling, the residue is filtered out, the liquid accurately neutralized with sodic hydrate and made up to 500 c. c. It is then titrated as usually, and can be calculated to glucose or starch on any basis desired. Thorough previous extraction and uninterrupted boiling are the two most important conditions. Without extraction the results are most uncertain and unreliable.

Determination of tannin.—The amount of tannin in certain spices, such as cloves and allspice, is quite constant when they are of good quality. Dr. Ellis of Toronto has therefore recommended this as a good means of detecting adulteration in these spices. He has published as yet nothing in regard to his methods of application. In our experiments it has been found to be of some value, but that it is hardly worth while as a mere aid to the detection of adulteration to go so far as the actual determination of tannin, it being quite sufficient to determine the amount of material oxidizable with permanganate which is extracted by water after the careful removal of the oil, &c., by ether. This avoids the tedious use of hide powder, or glue, and furnishes results which are relatively of the same value.

The analyst should therefore prepare himself for carrying out the first part of the modified Löwenthal process, as it is described in Sutton,* and more elaborately in the Berichte über die Verhandlungen der Commission zur Bestellung einer einheitliche Methode der Gerbstoffbestimmung, and in Annales de la Science agronomique, Tome 1, 1886.

Particular pains should be taken to secure a good article of indigo carmine, as without this the results are unreliable. That recommended by Schröder is manufactured by Gehe & Co., of Dresden, and is known as *Carminum cœruleum*. It should be imported for use.

Without going into particulars as to the reagents employed in the process, which are probably familiar to all, a few words of caution as to detail of manipulation will be of value.

As has been said, preliminary extraction of the material with Squibbs best ether is necessary to remove oil and other substances not tannin, on which the permanganate may act. Ordinary ether will not answer,

* Sutton, Volumetric Analysis, 3d edition, pp. 276.

as it contains so much alcohol and water as to dissolve some of the tannin. The substance freed from ether should be extracted with boiling water, and the extract made up to such dilution that 10 c. c. is equal to about 10 c. c. of the thirtieth normal permanganate solution used. The titration must be performed slowly to insure accuracy, the permanganate being run in at a rate of not more than a drop in a second or three in two seconds. The eye must become accustomed to the bleaching of the indigo and select some one tint of yellow as the end of reaction. It is then possible to obtain duplicates agreeing within .1 c. c. even on entirely different tests, as the following figures show:

Serial No.	C. c. of Perm.	Per ct. of tannin.
4904	4.33	22.46
	4.3	22.36
	4.35	22.62
	4.15	21.58

The results may be calculated to oxygen consumed or to percentage of quercitannic acid, which would not be strictly correct, 1 c. c. of $\frac{N}{30}$ permanganate being equivalent to .0052 grams of quercitannic acid. The results obtained with cloves and allspice will be found under those spices.

Crude fiber.—This is a merely relative determination, as the term crude fiber designates nothing absolute beyond the fact that a certain amount of substance is insoluble in acid and alkali of certain strength after treatment for a definite length of time at a definite temperature. The conditions selected by us are, 2 grams of substance, 200 c. c. of 5 per cent. hydrochloric acid, steam bath two hours, raising the liquid to a temperature of 90° to 95° C., filtration on linen cloth, washing back into beaker with 200 c. c. 5 per cent. sodic hydrate, steam bath two hours, filtration on asbestos, washing with hot water, alcohol, and ether, drying at 120° weighing, ignition and crude fiber from loss in weight. This method agrees practically with that known as the Weende method, and while furnishing results which are of some comparative value, leaves much to be desired. The subject will probably be reviewed soon by the Association of Official Agricultural Chemists of the United States.

Nitrogen and albuminoids.—The methods of determining nitrogen and albuminoids have been discussed and described at length in Bulletin No. 12 of this division. The details of the method of Kjeldahl, as given by Dr. Jenkins, which is the most convenient, are as follows:

Determination of nitrogen by the method of Kjeldahl.

REAGENTS AND APPARATUS.

(1) Hydrochloric acid whose absolute strength has been determined, (a) by precipitating with silver nitrate and weighing the silver chloride, (b) by sodium carbonate, as described in Fresenius's Quantitative Analysis, second American edition, page 680,

and (c) by determining the amount neutralized by the distillate from a weighed quantity of pure ammonium chloride boiled with an excess of sodium hydrate.

(2) Standard ammonia whose strength, relative to the acid, has been accurately determined.

(3) "C. P." sulphuric acid, Sp. Gr. 1.83, free from nitrates and also from ammonium sulphate, which is sometimes added in the process of manufacture to destroy oxides of nitrogen.

(4) Mercuric ox'de, HgO, prepared in the wet way. That prepared from mercury nitrate cannot safely be used.

(5) Potassium permanganate tolerably finely pulverized.

(6) Granulated zinc.

(7) A solution of 40 grams of commercial potassium sulphide in one liter of water-

(8) A saturated solution of sodium hydrate free from nitrates, which are sometimes added in the process of manufacture to destroy organic matter and improve the color of the product.

(9) Solution of cochineal prepared according to Fresenius's Quantitative Analysis, second American edition, page 679.

(10) Burettes should be calibrated in all cases by the user.

(11) Digestion flasks of hard, moderately thick, well-annealed glass. These flasks are about 9 inches long, with a round, pear-shaped bottom, having a maximum diameter of 2½ inches, and tapering out gradually in a long neck, which is three-fourth of an inch in diameter at the narrowest part, and flared a little at the edge. The total capacity is 225 to 250 cubic centimeters.

(12) Distillation flasks of ordinary shape, 550 cubic centimeters' capacity, and fitted with a rubber stopper and a bulb tube above to prevent the possibility of sodium hydrate being carried over mechanically during distillation. This is adjusted to the tube of the condenser by a rubber tube.

(13) A condenser. Several forms have been described, no one of which is equally convenient for all laboratories. The essential thing is that the tube which carries the steam to be condensed shall be of block tin. All kinds of glass are decomposed by steam and ammonia vapor, and will give up alkali enough to impair accuracy. (See Kreussler and Henzold, Ber. Berichte, *XVII*, 34.) The condenser in use in the laboratory of the Conn. Exp. Station, devised by Professor Johnson, consists of a copper tank supported by a wooden frame, so that its bottom is 11 inches above the work-bench on which it stands. This tank is 16 inches high, 32 inches long, and 3 inches wide from front to back, widening above to 6 inches. It is provided with a water-supply tube which goes to the bottom and a larger overflow pipe above. The block-tin condensing tubes, whose external diameter is ⅜ of an inch, 7 in number, enter the tank through holes in the front side of it near the top, above the level of the overflow, and pass down perpendicularly through the tank and out through rubber stoppers tightly fitted into holes in the bottom. They project about 1½ inches below the bottom of the tank, and are connected by short rubber tubes with glass bulb tubes of the usual shape, which dip into glass precipitating beakers. These beakers are 6½ inches high, 3 inches in diameter below, somewhat narrower above, and of about 500 cubic centimeters capacity. The titration can be made directly in them. The seven distillation flasks are supported on a sheet-iron shelf attached to the wooden frame that supports the tank in front of the latter. Where each flask is to stand a circular hole is cut, with three projecting lips, which support the wire gauze under the flask, and three other lips which hold the flask in place and prevent its moving laterally out of place while distillation is going on. Below this sheet-iron shelf is a metal tube carrying seven Bunsen burners, each with a stop-cock like those of a gas combustion furnace. These burners are of larger diameter at the top, which prevents smoking when covered with fine gauze to prevent the flame from striking back.

(14) The stand for holding the digestion flasks consists of a pan of sheet-iron 29 inches long by 8 inches wide, on the front of which is fastened a shelf of sheet-iron

as long as the pan, 5 inches wide and 4 inches high. In this are cut six holes 1⅝ inches in diameter. At the back of the pan is a stout wire running lengthwise of the stand, 8 inches high, with a bend or depression opposite each hole in the shelf. The digestion flask rests with its lower part over a hole in the shelf and its neck in one of the depressions in the wire frame, which holds it securely in position. Heat is supplied by low Bunsen burners below the shelf. Dr. Jenkins has used asbestus paper under the flasks, but finds that with a little care the naked flame can be applied directly to the flask without danger.

THE DETERMINATION.

One gram of the substance to be analyzed is brought into a digestion flask with approximately 0.7 gram of mercuric oxide and 20 cubic centimeters of sulphuric acid. The flask is placed on the frame above described in an inclined position and heated below the boiling point of the acid for from five to fifteen minutes, or until frothing has ceased. The heat is then raised till the acid boils briskly. No further attention is required till the contents of the flask has become a clear liquid, which is colorless or at least has only a very pale straw color. The flask is then removed from the frame, held upright, and while still hot, potassium permanganate is dropped in carefully and in small quantity at a time till after shaking the liquid remains of a green or purple color. After cooling, the contents of the flask are transferred to the distilling flask with water, and to this 25 cubic centimeters of potassium sulphide solution are added, 50 cubic centimeters of the soda solution, or sufficient to make the reaction strongly alkaline, and a few pieces of granulated zinc. The flask is at once connected with the condenser and the contents of the flask are distilled till all ammonia has passed over into the standard acid contained in the precipitating flask previously described and the concentrated solution can no longer be safely boiled. This operation usually requires from twenty to forty minutes. The distillate is then titrated with standard ammonia.

The use of mercuric oxide in this operation greatly shortens the time necessary for digestion, which is rarely over an hour and a half in the case of substances most difficult to oxidize and is more commonly less than an hour. In most cases the use of potassium permanganate is quite unnecessary, but it is believed that in exceptional cases it is required for complete oxidation, and in view of the uncertainty it is always used. Potassium sulphide removes all mercury from solution and so prevents the formation of mercuro-ammonium compounds which are not completely decomposed by soda solution. The addition of zinc gives rise to an evolution of hydrogen and prevents violent bumping. Previous to use the reagents should be tested by a blank experiment with sugar, which will partially reduce any nitrates that are present which might otherwise escape notice.

This method cannot be used for the determination of nitrogen in substances which contain nitrates or certain albuminoids.

In case non-albuminoid nitrogen is to be determined reference can be made to Stutzer and Ladd.*

These methods of analysis are suitable to all the spices and have been used with them. They are nothing but general processes, and are dependent for their value on uniformity in the way they are carried out and the manner in which peculiarities of proximate composition in different spices are considered in drawing conclusions. Determinations of particular substances, such as piperine, require, however, modifications, which must be described when discussing the analyses of each spice.

* Rept. anal. Chem., **5**, 162, 163; Abs. Ber., **19**, 1885; and Ladd Rept. of New York Agric. Exp. Sta., 1886.

Mustard of commerce is the seed, whole or ground, of several species of the genus *Brassica*, cruciferous plants which grow wild and are cultivated under very various conditions. The two common varieties are the black or brown mustard, which has a very small seed and furnishes the most aroma, and the white, which is two or three times as large, often used in the whole condition in pickles and ground, either by itself or oftener in mixture with the brown seed, for the purpose of obtaining the desirable qualities of both.

In the ground mustard is found only the interior of the seed and small portions of the husks which have escaped the operation of bolting, which is always employed to remove the coarse fragments. The presence of these particles from their characteristic structure enable us to recognize the source from which the flour is derived and to detect the use of the mustard hulls as adulterants of other food materials. The husk of white mustard is represented, after a drawing by Schimper, in Fig. 10.

The outer colorless epidermis consists of angular plates or hexagonal tabular cells with a center of different brilliancy. They swell up and become slimy in water and must therefore, be observed in glycerine. At the best it requires some manipulation to see it well, and it is far less prominent in the brown seed. The next coat, denominated the subepidermal, is not prominent and can only be seen at all easily in the white seed.

The third layer is an important one. In it is found the coloring matter of the brown seed, and its absence is the cause of the lack of color in the white variety. Fragments of this layer are common in ground mustard. It is distinguished by the thick or colorless brown cell walls and their irregular dotted appearance. Once examined it will be readily recognized under other circumstances, as, for example, when the hull is used as an adulterant of pepper.

Between this layer and the next are some unimportant and difficultly discernible cells carrying in the brown seed some color.

Within these comes the important layer denominated the inner tunic by Hassall and the plasma layer by Schimper. It separates readily from the other parts of the husk and is often found by itself in the ground mustard. As its contents are broken up by water or chloral hydrate, glycerine or oil must be used as a mounting medium. The cells of which the layer consists are large, and with their contents are similar to the embryous envelope or false gluten cells of wheat, to which they correspond. They are much alike in both white and brown mustard. These structures are diagramatically represented in Fig. 7.

From the character of the exterior layer and the lack of color in the third layer, as well as minor differences which are not describable, but will appear to the patient investigator, it is always possible to tell whether the flour of mustard is a mixture of the two varieties or from one alone. Mounts in chloral hydrate, to a certain degree, are useful for adding to the transparency of the substance. The interior of the seed is made up of small soft parenchyma cells containing the oil and other constituents of the mustard, but without any trace of starch. For this reason the presence of starch is a certain indication of the addition of some diluent of a farinaceous nature. Simple treatment with iodine will therefore reveal the presence of wheat flour, which is a common adulterant of this condiment. The white color of the flour of course reduces the yellow color of the mustard, and it is usual, therefore, to restore the tint by either *turmeric* or *Martin's yellow*.

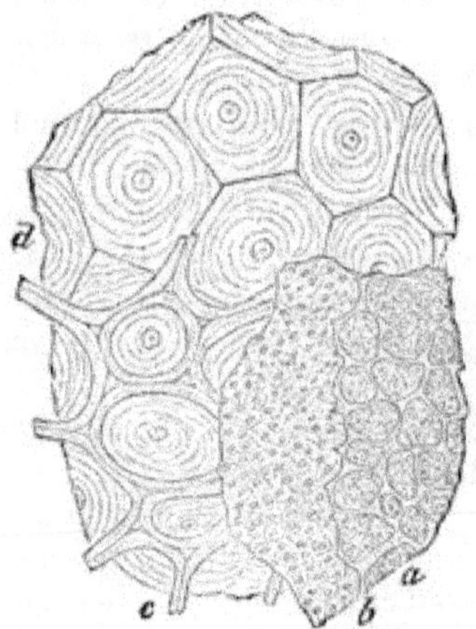

FIG. 16. Husk of white mustard. *a*, *b*, plasma layer; *c*, sub-epidermal; *d*, epidermis.

The former can be detected by a mechanical separation or a brown coloration with ammonia or by the peculiar color cells which it contains and the starch granules of the arrowroot class. The latter is not sufficient in amount to be confused with potato starch or that of flour. It has been already described.

Martin's yellow can be identified by extraction with cold 95 per cent. alcohol and examination, after evaporation of the solvent, as suggested by Waller and Martin, and this coloring matter seems to be often used, and cannot be pronounced as harmless as turmeric.

The substances mentioned are the common adulterants of mustard, in fact, so common that they have been accepted as necessary diluents, being considered desirable for toning down the pungency and adding to the keeping qualities of the ground material. Of late years, however, a reaction has taken place, and it is now possible to find brands of pure ground mustard.

In most of the samples which have come into our hands for examination flour and coloring matter are the only foreign substances which have been met with. From the investigations of foods chemists abroad, it would appear on the authority of Hassall and others that other species of mustard seed, rape seed, cayenne pepper, ginger, potato flour, rice, pea flour, seed meals, and several mineral substances are frequently found in the mustards of commerce, a conclusion which we have found justified by the presence in some of the lower-grade mustards which have come into our hands of yellow corn, ginger, mustard hulls, gypsum, and sand. The presence of these adulterants, which is only too common in the cheaper article when sold in bulk and under no brand, can be determined by mechanical means and by their structure, which is quite different from that of the mustard, and by the starches, which characterize some of them, as already explained.

While the adulterants of mustard, therefore, are, owing to the characteristic structure of the seed, easily detected with the microscope, in cases where there is doubt, or where further information is desired as to the probable proportion of diluent, recourse must be had to determinations of the chemical constituents of the sample.

CHEMISTRY OF MUSTARD.

Several investigators have made proximate analyses of mustard. Hassall has collected the following in regard to its composition, and has also made several analyses of pure and adulterated samples:

Of these seeds no very complete quantitative analyses have as yet been made, although many highly important particulars have been ascertained respecting their composition; thus black or brown mustard, as it is now generally named, consists for the most part of *fixed oil*, *myronic acid* $C_{10}H_{19}NS_2O_{10}$, which is combined with potash, forming a *myronate of potash*, and which acid is converted into the volatile oil of mustard or *sulphocyanide of allyl* C_4H_5NS or $\left.\begin{matrix} CN \\ C_3H_5 \end{matrix}\right\} S$ through the agency of the *myrosin*, another constituent of brown mustard, when the two are brought into contact through the medium of water, *vegetable albumen*, a *bitter principle*, a little *gum* and *sugar*, *a peculiar green substance*, *cellulose* and *mineral matter*.

White mustard differs essentially in its composition from brown; it also contains *fixed oil*, but in lieu of myronic acid, convertible as described into the volatile oil of mustard, it contains a non-volatile, bitter and acrid salt, termed *sulphocyanide of synapine* ($C_{17}H_{24}N_2SO_8$ or $C_{16}H_{23}NO_5CNHS$), *myroxin*, *gum*, *cellulose*, *and mineral matter*.

Now it is on the volatile oil and the acrid and somewhat bitter salt that the pungency and acridity of mustard depends, and hence we see a strong reason why in the mustards of commerce the farina of the two species should be blended together; of the two active principles the volatile oil is by far the more important, and hence the seed of the brown mustard possesses the greatest commercial value. It should be stated that Henrie and Garot affirms that brown mustard contains the acrid principle as well as the white; this statement we have been able to verify as shown specially by the action of nitric acid, caustic potash, and ferric chloride on the alcoholic extract.

The acrid principle of white mustard appears to possess but little stability, and although it is stated by V. Babo to bear a temperature of 130°C., we find that it is readily affected by heat, and that it is not safe to evaporate the alcoholic solution containing it at a higher temperature than about 30°C. If subjected to a much higher temperature it quickly loses its acridity and acquires a bitter caramel-like taste.

Of neither brown nor white mustard had any percentage analysis been given until those made and published by ourselves in an article on mustard and its adulterations, in "Food, Water, and Air," for February, 1874; and in the few cases in which the quantities of any of the constituents are stated, they vary greatly according to different observers. Thus, according to Pereira, the *fixed oil* forms about 28 per cent. of the seeds of black mustard, while Watts puts the yield at 18 per cent. only, but white mustard seed, he says, furnishes 36 per cent. The *volatile oil* amounts to 0.20 per cent., according to Boutron and Robiquet; 0.55 per cent., according to Aschoff, and 0.50 per cent. according to Wittstock; all of which quantities are much below the mark, as will be seen hereafter. Now, as will be shown presently, there is little or no difference in the amount of fixed oil furnished by the two descriptions of mustard, that obtained by me from the farina of brown mustard reaching 35.701 per cent., and that from the white mustard 35.768 per cent. Again it is shown by the analyses given below that the volatile oil occurs in much larger quantities than those enumerated above, the amount which we have obtained from one sample being no less than 1.271 per cent.

Of both brown and white mustard we append the following original percentage analyses, first published in the article referred to:

BROWN MUSTARD FARINA.

	Per cent.
Water	4.845
Fixed oil	35.701
Myronic acid	4.840
Myrosin and albumen	29.536
Acrid salt	3.588
Cellulose	16.765
Ash	4.725
	100.000
Volatile oil	1.271
Nitrogen	5.068
Sulphur	1.413

The oil extracted by ether from the brown seed is of a bright and beautiful emerald green color, owing to the presence of the peculiar green principle described as one of its constituents. So deep and remarkable is the color of the oil that it would be easy, by means of a graduated scale of tints, to determine with very tolerable certainty the percentage of brown mustard contained in any samples of mixed mustard.

WHITE MUSTARD FARINA.

	Per cent.
Water	5.360
Fixed oil	35.768
Acrid salt	10.983
Myrosin and albumen	27.484
Cellulose	16.295
Ash	4.110
	100.000
Nitrogen	5.285
Sulphur	1.224

These analyses, whether regarded from a scientific or practical point of view, are possessed of much interest.

The small quantity of sugar found in mustard would, from the method of analysis pursued, be included under the bitter principle and the gum with cellulose.

Of the methods of analysis, Hassall writes:

Estimation of myronic acid.—Myronate of potash decomposes, under the influence of the nitrogenous matter contained in brown mustard, into volatile oil, glucose, and acid sulphate of potash. The quantity of each of these products of decomposition gives, therefore, by simple calculation, the quantity of myronic acid. One hundred parts of this acid yield 23.85 parts of volatile oil. From 40 to 50 grams of the mustard farina are placed in a flask of about one-half liter capacity; 250 c. c. of tepid water are poured over it, the flask closed with a cork, and the whole is well shaken. After twenty-four hours' standing the flask is connected with a Liebig's condenser, and its contents are heated to boiling. Into the receiver 30 c. c. of strong ammonia are poured, and the end of the condenser is dipped below the surface of the liquid. Water and the volatile oil pass over, the latter at first floating in the shape of oily drops on the surface of the liquid, which soon sink to the bottom, especially when the liquid is gently agitated. When the distillation is finished, which is the case when no more oil globules pass over, the receiver is closed with a cork and allowed to stand twenty-four hours. At the end of that time all the oil is dissolved and is now contained in the liquid in the form of thiosinnamin. This solution is evaporated on the water bath in a weighed platinum basin, the residue dried and weighed. The quantity of thiosinnamine obtained, minus one molecule of ammonia, represents the amount of volatile oil.

Estimation of the myrosin or albumen and of the sulphocyanide of sinapin.—The total amounts of nitrogen and sulphur contained in the mustard are next ascertained. The former by combustion with soda-lime in the well-known manner, the latter by deflagration of the mustard and oxidation of its sulphur in a mixture of nitrate of soda and carbonate of potash. The fused mass is dissolved in water or dilute acid, and the sulphuric acid contained in the solution is estimated by means of chloride of barium. From these data the amounts of the myrosin and of the sulphocyanide of sinapin, the acrid principle, are thus calculated; as much sulphur and nitrogen are first deducted from the totals of these substances obtained as is contained in the quantity of myronic acid previously determined. Next, the whole of the remaining sulphur and as much of the nitrogen as is required are then calculated into the acrid principle; lastly, the surplus nitrogen is calculated into myrosin, which has the same formula as vegetable albumen. But now, having got approximately the amounts of the acrid principle and of the myrosin, a further calculation has to be made, since myrosin contains about 1 per cent. of sulphur. This has to be deducted from the total acrid principle, a corresponding quantity of nitrogen being in its turn calculated into myrosin. By those acquainted with algebra it will readily be perceived that a more precise calculation may be made, but the results would not, even then, differ to any practical extent.

Acting on this method, Hassall made several analyses of genuine mustards of the trade and also of adulterated articles, which are here presented, merely dropping the third place in decimals, which is of no value.

Analyses of genuine mustard.

[Hassall, pp. 514-516.]

	Genuine mustard.	Genuine double superfine.	Genuine superfine.	Genuine Fine.	Pure.	House hold.
Water	5.70	5.16	5.39	5.68	5.08	5.79
Fixed oil	36.49	35.91	34.71	35.24	33.98	36.75
Myronic acid	2.70	2.21	1.97	.92	.96	1.72
Myrosin and albumen	31.69	27.36	31.02	27.90	27.62	8.75
Acrid salt and bitter principle	5.72	9.09	7.10	10.06	11.26	27.48
Cellulose	13.37	15.58	15.29	15.35	16.81	3.69
Ash	4.33	4.66	4.32	4.65	4.29	16.32
	100.00	100.00	100.00	100.00	100.00	100.00
Oil of mustard	.71	.58	.52	.24	.25	.45
Nitrogen	5.34	5.05	5.46	5.16	5.21	5.03
Sulphur	1.31	1.42	1.25	1.30	1.40	1.31

Analyses of mixed and bulk mustard.

	Double superfine.	Fine.	Superior.	Suerls.	Alexander.	Lindsey.	Gilbert.	Goodman.	Clark.
Water	4.94	6.51	4.97	8.91	8.34	8.87	6.28	8.95	9.58
Fixed oil	27.52	23.16	25.17	24.88	29.60	21.54	22.06	26.90	18.31
Myronic acid	3.14	1.36	1.20	1.57	1.02	.98	1.43	1.82	.39
Acrid principle	1.85	5.81	4.31	6.45	3.15	6.21	4.25	5.18	7.03
Myrosin	23.16	19.50	23.24	14.48	13.89	21.76	15.30	15.58	20.82
Wheat flour and turmeric.	22.99	27.20	25.82	33.84	30.52	25.21	38.82	30.56	32.81
Cellulose	13.05	12.81	11.50	7.08	8.99	11.09	8.41	7.27	8.65
Ash	3.35	3.62	3.79	3.79	3.59	3.74	3.75	3.74	2.41
Volatile oil	.85	.36	.32	.41	.50	.26	.30	.48	.10
Nitrogen	4.24	3.85	4.07	3.34	3.16	4.30	3.46	3.37	3.33
Sulphur	.95	.96	1.06	1.00	.90	.94	.82	.94	.91

"Of the first six analyses of genuine mustards" Hassall says that they "prove two things; first, that all the samples are genuine; this is shown by the quantities of fixed oil, nitrogen, and sulphur obtained; and that they consist of mixtures of the two mustards in different proportions, the higher qualities containing larger proportions of the brown mustard; that this is so is demonstrated by the different quantities of volatile oil obtained."

In the analyses of the adulterated mustards allowance in the calculation was made for the nitrogen of the wheat flour.

Hassall says:

From an examination of the foregoing analyses it is apparent that genuine *brown* mustard should contain about 36 per cent. of fixed oil, at least 1 per cent. of volatile oil of mustard, about 4 per cent. of acrid principle, and that it should furnish about 1.5 per cent. of sulphur and 5 per cent. of nitrogen; that genuine *white* mustard should yield about the same amount of fixed oil, over 10 per cent. of acrid principle, and nearly the same amount of nitrogen and sulphur as the black; that the composition of genuine mustards, which are made up in various proportions of brown and white mustard seed, differs according to the quantities of each kind present, the relative proportions being determinable by analysis with considerable precision; that in the mixed or adulterated mustards the proportions of fixed and volatile oil, of nitrogen, and sulphur are all much reduced, according to the extent of the admixtures, these consisting in the mustards now reported upon in all cases of wheat flour and turmeric.

Thus the fixed oil was reduced in one of the samples from 36 per cent., the normal amount, to about one-half or 18 per cent., the volatile oil to 0.1 per cent., and the nitrogen to 3.32 per cent., while in another sample the sulphur was as low as 0.81 per cent. The amount of wheat flour and turmeric varied from 22.91 per cent. to 38.82 per cent., that is to say, from one-fourth to one-third of the article.

These results furnish an excellent basis for the examination of the mustards met with in our country. In addition, however, we have the work of several other investigators. C. H. Piesse and Lionel Stansell* have given their results of the analyses of several samples of pure farinas and their ashes, largely after the method of Hassall. Blyth copies them,† and adds several pages on the chemistry of mustard and its adulterations, adding nothing new to what has been quoted from Hassall, with the exception of a formula for calculating the percentage of added flour in mixtures from the amount of fixed oil found. He says:

Estimation of fat or oil.—This is particularly useful when wheat starch is the adulterating agent. Wheat flour does not contain more than 1.2 to 2.1 per cent. of oil; mustard, on the other hand, from 33.9 to 36.7 per cent. A weighed portion of the previously dried samples may be placed in an extraction apparatus, and from the oil found the following formulæ will serve as a guide to the amount of flour present:

x = amount of mustard, y = amount of oil found.

$$\frac{33.9\,x}{100}+\frac{1.2\,(100-x)}{100}=y \qquad \frac{36.7\,x}{100}+\frac{2\,(100-x)}{100}=y$$

according as the greater or less amount of oil is taken as being present in the pure farina and the flour.

Accepting the mean for mustard and 2.0 per cent. as the proper figure for flour, the formula would read more conveniently, it would seem,

$$x=\frac{y-2}{1.333}$$

where $x=100$ when the mustard is pure. Of the amount of ash Blyth says:

"The total ash of dried mustard averages 5 per cent. The highest number the writer has obtained is 5.3 per cent.; the lowest 5.088 per cent. Of this ash 1.2 at least is soluble in water; in other words, the ash of mustard consists of 30 parts per cent. soluble, 70 parts per cent. insoluble in water. It hence follows that if found above 5.5 per cent. mineral matters of foreign origin are present; if below 4 per cent. it is an indication of some organic adulterant."

Albert R. Leeds and Edgar Everhart‡ have taken up Hassall's and Blyth's work and shown that the latter's formula for calculating added flour from the percentage of oil found will not serve in all cases, as it is not uncommon to express some of the oil from the seed before grinding, to adulterate with oil cake or seeds, or to add cheap oils to the flour used as a diluent to cover any deficiency. They also analyzed a sample of pure farina of brown mustard according to a method devised by themselves as a modification of Hassall, in which the determinations should be direct instead of calculated. Briefly, it is as follows:

* Analyst, **5**, 161-165, 1880.

† Foods and their adulterations, 485-486.

‡ Zeit. anal. Chem. **21**, 389-394, 1882.

Moisture and ash are determined as usual; oil, in a portion of mustard dried at 105°, by ether in an extraction apparatus, with subsequent drying at 100°. From the dried residue the *sulphocyanide of sinapin* and the *myronate of potassium* are extracted in a similar way by 50 per cent. alcohol. The extract is dried, weighed, and ignited, and from the sulphate of potash in the ash the myronate is reckoned and the sulphocyanide obtained by difference. The residue, containing *myrosin* and *cellulose* and a little coloring matter, is freed from alcohol and treated with one-half per cent. sodic hydrate solution. The washed residue is weighed and ignited for cellulose. The filtrate containing all the myrosin is nearly neutralized with dilute hydrochloric acid, 50 c. c. of Ritthausen's copper sulphate solution added, and then dilute sodic hydrate to near neutrality. The heavy green myrosin copper compound is filtered off, dried at 110° C., weighed, and ignited. The difference is the myrosin.

Analyses carried out after this method in triplicate are as follows:

	Per cent.	Per cent.	Per cent.
Water	6.78	6.90	6.82
Myronate of potash	.61	.61	.72
Sulpho-cyanide of sinapine	10.97	11.19	11.21
Myrosin	28.45	28.70	28.30
Oil	29.22	29.21	29.19
Cellulose (by difference)	20.24	19.55	20.06
Ash	3.73	3.84	3.70

The amounts of nitrogen and sulphur in this mustard were:

Nitrogen 5.337
Sulphur 1.489

Calculated from these figures according to the method of Hassall would be found the following:

Myronate of potassium .... .61
Sulphocyanide of sinapine 10.71
Myrosin 28.52

Showing a close agreement with the direct determinations.

Direct methods are, however, usually preferable and this would, no doubt, be a good one were it not that dilute alcohol in the case of admixture of flour would dissolve so much of the albuminoid matter and ash of the latter as to invalidate the determination of myronate. It is therefore open to criticism.

E. Waller and E. W. Martin * in 1882 made an examination of mustards manufactured and sold in New York City, attention being paid to moisture, oil, and soluble and insoluble ash. They also examined mustard pastes, and compared their results with some pure mustards from the English market. Their analyses are as follows:

* Analyst 9, 166-170.

Dry mustard manufactured and sold in New York City.

No.	Moisture.	Fixed oil.	Soluble ash.	Insoluble ash.	Total.	Coloring.	Remarks.
197	6.15	21.17	.30	5.54	5.84	Martin's yellow..	Contains starch.
204	8.03	12.79	1.39	5.39	6.78	Turmeric	Contains starch and Ca SO_4.
206	7.35	12.54	.23	4.69	4.92	......do	Ash fixed starch.
207	8.23	8.42	.15	1.90	2.05	Martin's yellow...	Contains starch.
208	8.50	10.92	2.90	13.15	16.05	Turmeric	Contains starch, Ca SO_4.
209	7.24	6.81	.10	3.55	3.65	......do	Contains starch
213	7.65	13.32	.64	5.17	5.81	Martin's yellow...	Contains starch, ash-fused.
214	7.60	7.74	1.53	1.69	3.22	Turmeric	Contains starch.
215	7.15	9.02	.20	2.91	3.11	......do	Contains starch.
216	5.45	20.37	.15	5.12	5.27	......do	Contains starch.
217	6.50	8.59	1.52	5.65	8.17	......do	Contains starch, Ca SO_4.
218	8.45	14.59	2.15	6.65	8.80	......do	Contains starch, Ca SO_4.
219	6.62	22.56	1.62	4.86	6.48	....	No starch.
294	9.86	6.21	1.16	3.54	4.70	Martin's yellow...	

Mustard paste, German mustard manufactured in New York City.

No.	Moisture.	Acetic acid.	Oil.	Other organic substance.	Soluble ash.	Insoluble ash.	Total.	Common salt.	Oil on dry substance.	Metallic copper.
221	77.02	2.76	2.55	14.18	2.51	0.93	3.49	2.11	24.98	.001
222	81.52	1.98	3.50	10.67	1.77	.56	2.33	1.63	21.24	Trace.
237	79.62	2.43	3.90	12.60	2.52	.97	3.49	....	19.51	.009
242	76.54	3.69	4.57	11.53	2.69	.98	3.67	1.86	23.14	.003
244	81.45	2.94	3.73	9.09	2.14	.65	2.79	1.77	22.44	Trace.

Mustard flour (bolted) purporting to be pure.

No.	Moisture.	Oil.	Soluble ash.	Insoluble ash.	Total.	Remarks.
201	6.10	26.42	.29	5.92	6.21	New York manufacture.
220	5.50	25.70	.86	4.80	5.66	New York manufacture, Trieste and Bombay seed, mixed.
273	4.85	36.67	.175	3.725	3.900	English samples, whole seed.
274	4.75	41.70	.125	4.425	4.550	English samples, brown seed, ash-fused.

Ground mustard seeds.

No.	Kind of seed.	Moisture.	Oil.	Soluble ash.	Insoluble ash.	Total.
	American market:					
231	Bombay	7.52	36.96	1.25	4.37	5.62
232	Trieste	6.35	36.45	.70	3.70	4.40
233	California yellow	4.95	34.00	.50	4.40	4.90
234	English yellow	6.10	35.46	.25	4.55	4.80
	English market:					
271	White	7.10	34.43	.70	3.90	4.60
272	Brown	7.30	34.71	.85	3.90	4.75

As comment they say:

The results obtained for oil on Nos. 201 and 220 led to inquiry, the result of which was the discovery that it is the regular practice of the mustard manufacturers here to express a portion of the oil from the ground mustard seed before working it up into the condiment sold as mustard. In these samples, as well as in No. 219, which was sold under guarantee of being pure mustard without admixture, no starch, coloring material, or other material known to be foreign to the mustard seed was found.

If we calculate, then, that these mustards have been made up from mustard flour similar to 201 and 220, and containing 25 per cent. of oil, by multiplying the percentages of oil given in the table by four, we shall get approximately the proportions of mustard flour present, in percentages.

These investigators also examined a specimen of English mustard which was mixed with starch, and yet contained a normal amount of oil which, on extraction, was decidedly more fluid than mustard oil. This points to the truth of the assertion that the extraction of the mustard oil is often covered by the addition of oil of inferior character.

The common use of Martin's yellow (Dinitronapthol) as a coloring matter is startling, as it can hardly be anything but injurious. They detected it by extracting the flour with cold, strong alcohol, evaporating, taking up with water and dyeing wool with it. Crystals, however, could not be obtained, but the authors came into possession of a sample of the coloring matter which was analyzed.

In Canada, large numbers of samples of mustard have been examined with results which have already been quoted, showing that the manufacture of mustard from mustard cake and the addition of farinaceous matter is as common there as elsewhere. In the report for 1885, out of fifty-one specimens, only 10 contained over 25 per cent. of fixed oil and no starch, and but three contained over 30 per cent. oil, as they should, if of best quality. The chief analyst, however, is of the opinion that the removal of the oil is an advantage, as the flour will keep better and be as pungent without it.

With the information of the nature which has been given a number of samples of mustard purchased in the open market in Washington, some of low grade obtained direct from Baltimore spice mills, and others in the whole seed from the importers and dealers, have been examined microscopically and chemically. They may be described as follows:

Serial No.	Price ½ pound (retail).	Remarks.
	Cents.	
4510	....	White seed.
11	30	Guaranteed pure.
22	20	Ground in District of Columbia.
27	20	Ground in Baltimore.
32	30	English brand.
36	36	Ground in Baltimore.
42	30	English brand.
50	20	
51	20	Ground in New York.
4211	....	Mohawk, N. Y.
71	....	Extra American, Baltimore, Md.
72	....	London, strong, extra, Baltimore, Md.
4971	20	Ground in Baltimore; extensively advertised as pure.
4885	....	White-seed flour, ground in laboratory.
86	....	White-seed husk, ground in laboratory.
99	....	California yellow mustard seed.
4900	....	California brown mustard seed.
1	....	English yellow mustard seed.
2	....	Trieste brown mustard seed.

The analytical determinations gave the following results:

Analyses of mustard.

[Whole-seed flour.]

Serial No.	Source.	Weight of 100 seeds, in grams.	Quality.	Water.	Ash.	Volatile oil.	Fixed oil.	Starch.	Crude fiber.	Albuminoids.	Undetermined.	Total.	Nitrogen.
4510	White seed	635		5.57	4.29	.97	33.56	.00	5.40	28.88	21.33	100	4.62
4885	White flour			3.33	5.23	1.84	34.83	.00	9.65	25.56	20.16	100	**4.09**
4886	Seed husk	480		6.17	4.99	.55	28.12	.00	9.50	23.44	27.23	100	3.75
4899	California yellow	460		4.83	5.96	1.27	31.96	.00	8.50	31.13	16.35	100	**4.98**
4900	California brown	135		4.11	4.88	1.35	36.63	.00	16.18	24.69	12.16	100	**3.95**
4901	English yellow	419		3.11	4.07	2.06	31.51	.00	6.90	30.25	22.10	100	**4.84**
4902	Trieste brown	425		4.62	5.61	.63	39.55	.00	10.84	25.88	18.87	100	**4.14**

[Commercial mustard flour.]

Serial No.	Source.	Weight of 100 seeds, in grams.	Quality.	Water.	Ash.	Volatile oil.	Fixed oil.	Starch.	Crude fiber.	Albuminoids.	Undetermined.	Total.	Nitrogen.
4511	(?)		Colored	5.97	6.55	.43	**18.16**	.00	7.35	**37.44**	24.10	100	**5.95**
4522	District of Columbia		Adulterated	9.38	7	.24	**11.20**	**21.15**	**2.95**	**20.63**	27.04	100	3.30
4527	Baltimore		do	9.73	4.40	.80	**9.85**	**29.14**	**2.10**	**13.31**	30.37	100	2.13
4532	English		do	5.84	4.90	2.11	**30.84**	**7.26**	4.63	25.88	18.54	100	4.14
4536	Baltimore		do	6.00	**9.70**	.50	**11.72**	**9.00**	**3.75**	**14.50**	41.23	100	3.92
4542	English		do	3.25	**3.65**	2.01	**32.26**	8.50	**14.98**	25.19	10.16	100	4.03
4550	(?)		do	5.89	**3.15**	.37	**7.89**	**40.50**	**2.13**	**14.38**	25.46	100	2.30
4551	New York		do	6.70	**1.90**	1.31	**3.50**	**15.00**	**2.97**	**13.63**	21.99	100	2.18
4871	Baltimore		do	4.57	**3.24**	2.02	**6.77**	**31.50**	**2.90**	**20.31**	28.60	100	3.25
4872	Baltimore		do	7.25	**3.35**	2.32	**5.54**	**34.63**	**1.23**	**19.63**	26.05	100	3.14
4971	Baltimore		do	6.03	5.98	.65	**19.46**	**5.70**	**3.18**	**33.06**	25.64	100	5.29

Abnormal figures in full-faced type.

DISCUSSION OF THE ANALYSES.

The results obtained with pure seed, ground in the laboratory, show that flour of mustard is fairly constant in its composition.

Water is present in small amount, as is generally the case in oil seeds, varying between 3 and 7 per cent. Hassall found from 5.16 to 5.70, and Waller and Martin 7.52 to 4.95.

Ash is quite constant between 4 and 6 per cent., so that the presence of foreign mineral matter is readily detected. Blyth places the variation between 5.1 and 5.3, Waller and Martin between 4.40 and 5.62, while in ground samples it falls as low as 2.05, Waller and Martin, or 1.90, our own results, owing to the addition of organic adulterants, such as wheat flour, or rises to 16 per cent. from the addition of gypsum. The determination is therefore an extremely valuable one.

Volatile oil is present naturally in the seed in but small amount. The percentage we have found to be rather variable, as much as 2.06 having been found in an English yellow seed and as little as .55 in another. Hassall found from .71 to 24 per cent. Its presence is not of importance.

Fixed oil is one of the most prominent constituents of the seed, varying in amount from 31 to 37 per cent. Waller and Martin give results varying from 34 to 37, and Hassall 34.71 to 36.49. It has become an almost universal practice, however, to express a portion of the oil, so that in good flour as little as 18 per cent. has been found.

Starch is entirely absent, a contrast to the cereal grains and many other seeds. Its addition is of course common.

Crude fiber varies in a way dependent on the method of milling and of determining its amount. Our samples were found to contain much more than the best flour of commerce, as our means of separating the husk are imperfect. With careful milling not more than 6 to 7 per cent. should be present, according to modern chemical methods. Hassall, on the other hand, found from 13 to 17 per cent.

Albuminoids make up a large part of the seed, varying from 25 to 32 per cent. Anything below 20 per cent. points to dilution with material poor in nitrogen.

The *undetermined* matter consists of gum and some unidentified substances soluble in alcohol, whose estimation is of no particular value as a means of detecting adulteration.

Our results, as a whole, agree closely with those of other investigators, so that for general reference the following standard may be used:

	Per. cent.
Water	3 to 7
Ash	4 6
Volatile oil	½ 2
Fixed oil:	
When from entire seed.	31 37
When from cake	16 18
Starch	None.
Crude fiber	5 18
Albuminoids	25 32

When, however, the flour is ground from cake all the percentages may be somewhat increased.

As compared with the pure mustards the flours of commerce give results which show at once the universal extent of the adulteration which takes place, aside from any microscopic examination.

4511, purchased in Washington but ground elsewhere, has been deprived of nearly half of its fixed oil, that is to say, is ground from mustard cake. It is the only specimen which contains no farinaceous material, and is higher in albuminoids than any of the pure seeds or flours. This is due to the fact that abstraction of the oil raises the relative percentage of albuminoids, and this is not reduced at all by the addition of any diluent. The amount of fiber is relatively high for the same reason. It contains also a very small amount of mineral adulteration. The microscope shows the presence of turmeric as coloring matter.

This brand is perhaps the purest met with, as its only defects are lack of, oil which has been considered not a loss, the small amount mineral matter, and the presence of a little coloring matter.

4522, represented by two different specimens, has, in one case, that analyzed, been deprived of more oil than the preceding, has a considerable amount of gypsum in its ash, and 21 per cent. of starch in the shape of wheat flour. The relative percentages of fiber and albuminoids are thereby reduced somewhat, since 21 per cent. of starch would correspond to about 30 per cent. of flour. Color is given by turmeric. In the other case the changes were similar, except that no turmeric was added, but large amounts of white mustard hulls.

4527, ground in Baltimore, consists to a large extent of flour, between 40 and 50 per cent., and is made from mustard cake, the oil having been removed. The color has been restored by turmeric. The sample leaves on sieving quite a large amount of husky and fibrous matter contaminated with wheat flour and turmeric. The husks are not those of the original mustard, and have not been identified, but seem to resemble the exterior coats of ginger, and may represent an addition of spent ginger or ginger tailing.

4522, sieving leaves white mustard hulls and yellow corn meal, but no color; wheat flour is also present.

4531. This sample contains turmeric, wheat flour, and salt.

4532. An English brand, is made from whole seed and is diluted with but little flour and color, about 10 per cent. of the former.

4536 is made from mustard cake, contains a large amount of gypsum and some starch, and is colored (with turmeric). The large amount of undetermined matter would point also to the presence of other adulterants not identified.

4542 resembles the other English brand examined, 4532 being only altered by the addition of a little flour and color.

4550 and 4551 are perhaps the worst samples we have examined. They are made from cake, contain no mineral adulterants, but are more than half flour, and are of course much colored with turmeric. They were purchased from the same grocery. One also contained salt, detected by sifting.

4871 and 4872 are similar and but little superior. They were obtained directly from a Baltimore mill in a lot of spices, which were all adulterated.

4971 has been much advertised as quite pure, but was found to contain sand and flour, but no color. It is made, as usual, from seed cake. From these samples we learn the quality of the ordinary flour mustard of the groceries. It is not good, and certainly demands reform.

PEPPER.

The ordinary black and white peppers of commerce are the fruit of the true pepper plant, *Piper nigrum*, which grows in the East and West Indies. Red pepper, or cayenne, is not a pepper, but the fruit of several species of *Capsicum*. Under the title of "pepper," therefore, attention will be confined to the genus *Piper*, reserving for a separate chapter the remaining substances which are commonly miscalled peppers.

The pepper plant is a perennial climbing shrub, with a small, round, sessile, fleshy fruit, which grows spontaneously on the Malabar coast, and whose culture has been extended to Siam, Hindostan, Indo-China, Malacca, Singapore, Penang, Ceylon, Sumatra, Java, Borneo, and the neighboring islands, and to a small extent in Guiana and Cayenne.

The greatest production is in Sumatra, and the ports of export are principally Singapore and Penang, the Malabar pepper coming from Tellicherry. Our imports are principally through England, and not direct, and it seems that, in England at least, it is customary to mix peppers of different origin in grinding, taking Malabar for weight, Penang for strength, and Sumatra for color.

Of the other characteristics and history of pepper a most complete account may be found in "Flückiger and Hanbury's Pharmacographia."* Of its preparation for the market these authors say:

When one or two berries at the base of the spike begin to turn red the whole spike is pinched off. Next day the berries are rubbed off with the hands and picked clean, then dried for three days on mats or on smooth, hard ground or on bamboo baskets near a gentle fire.

As thus prepared it is the black pepper of the trade.

When the berries are allowed to ripen, and the black outer pericarp is removed on drying, they are known as white pepper.

The grains of white pepper are of rather larger size than those of black, and of a warm, grayish tint. They are nearly spherical or a little flattened. At the base the skin of the fruit is thickened into a blunt prominence, whence about twelve light stripes run meridian-like toward the depressed summit. If the skin is scraped off the dark-brown testa is seen inclosing the hard, translucent albumen. In anatomical structure, as well as in taste and smell, white pepper agrees with black, which, in fact, it represents in a rather more fully-grown state.

A study of the structure of black pepper will, therefore, furnish every information in regard to the white. There are also two species of *Piper* which furnish a berry used in a similar way to that of *Piper nigrum*. They are known as long pepper, *Piper longum* and *Piper officinarum*. Their structure is similar to that of the common pepper, with some characteristic differences. It is difficult to say how far they are an article of commerce in this country. They come principally from Penang and Singapore, being brought from Java and other places.

The structure of black pepper is described as follows in the work last quoted:

The small, round berry-like fruits grow somewhat loosely to the number of twenty to thirty on a common pendulous fruit stalk. They are at first green, then become red, and, if allowed to ripen, yellow, but they are gathered before complete maturity, and by drying in that state turn blackish gray or brown. If left until quite ripe they lose some of their pungency and gradually fall off.

The berries after drying are spherical, about one-fifth inch in diameter, wrinkled on the surface, indistinctly pointed below by the remains of a very short pedicel, and

* London, McMillan & Co., 1879.

crowned still more indistinctly by the three or four lobed stigma. The thin pericarp tightly encloses a single seed, the embryo of which, in consequence of premature gathering, is undeveloped and merely replaced by a cavity situated below the apex. The seed itself contains within the thin red-brown testa a shining albumen, gray and horny without and mealy within. The pungent taste and peculiar smell of pepper are familiar to all.

The transverse section of the grain of black pepper exhibits a soft yellowish epidermis, covering the outer pericarp. This is formed of a closely-packed yellow layer of large, mostly radially arranged, thick-walled cells, each containing in its small cavity a mass of dark brown resin. The middle layer of the pericarp consists of soft tangentially extended parenchyme, containing an abundance of extremely small starch granules and drops of oil. The shrinking of this loose middle layer is the chief cause of the deep wrinkles on the surface of the berry. The next inner layer of the pericarp exhibits towards its circumference tangentially arranged, soft parenchyme, the cells of which possess either spiral striation or spiral fibers, but towards the interior loose parenchyme free from starch and containing very large oil cells. The testa is formed in the first place of a row of small yellow thick-walled cells. Next to them follows the true testa, as a dense, dark brown layer of lignified cells, the individual outlines of which are indistinguishable. The albumen of the seeds consists of angular, radially arranged, large-celled parenchyme. Most of its cells are colorless and loaded with starch, others contain a soft yellow amorphous mass. If thin slices are kept under glycerine for some time, these masses are slowly transformed into needle-shaped crystals of piperin.

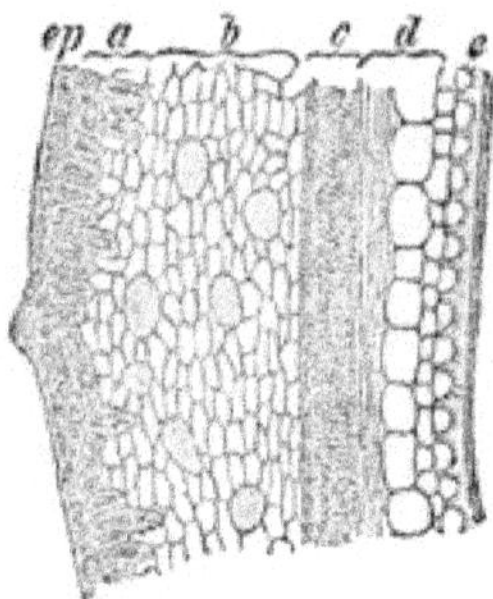

FIG. 11. Pepper husk, cross-section. *ep*, epidermis; *a*, stone cells; *b*, parenchyme with oil cells; *c*, spiral vessels; *d*, inner parenchyme; *e*, inner layer of stone cells. (After Schimper.)

Of the structure described so well in the preceding lines, of a portion of which a diagramatic illustration is given in Fig. 11, after Schimper, only parts are readily found in the powdered pepper of the shops. The angular cells of the interior of the seed are of course the most prominent, and when once seen their characteristic form and contents are easily recognized again. The structure of the outer coats is made out with more difficulty. It is well, before attempting to do so on a ground pepper, to soften some whole black and white pepper-corns in glycerine and cut sections from various parts of the exterior of the berry. Taking the white pepper first it will not be found difficult in such sections mounted in glycerine to pick out three layers of different cells composing the outer coat of the corn, beside the angular large cells of the interior, which are filled with starch and piperine, the latter being yellow in color. The first of these layers and outer one is made up of colorless large loosely-arranged cells, with some fibers, more compact toward the exterior than the interior of the layer and carrying globules of oil. This layer makes up the principal part of the husk of white pepper. The second layer is a part of what Flückiger calls the testa, and consists of small yellow cells, thick walled and closely appressed. Next the third layer and second portion of the testa consists of liginified brown cells, which in their transverse appearance resemble some of the cells of mustard hulls, the individuality not being made out easily owing to the thickness of the walls. Having become thoroughly familiar with these appearances the white ground pepper should be examined and will be found to differ in the way in which these coats are presented. They can be recognized, however, and must be studied until thoroughly understood. The presence of the least portion of adulterant is then readily detected.

The black pepper is not as simple in its arrangement as the white. The maturity of the latter gives its structure more distinctness, while in the black the more or less shrunken character of the berry renders the recognition of the various tissues difficult. In a section from the exterior of a softened black pepper the interior coats, after what has been learned with the white, will be quickly recognized, but will be found to not be as plainly developed. The coats of the outer pericarp, which in the white pepper were wanting, will be found to be dark-colored, shrunken, and confused, so that it will require much study to discover the forms of cell which Flückiger describes. It will be found easier, perhaps, in the ground black pepper. There the structures already recognized in the ground white pepper will be seen and in addition dark-brown particles, portions of the outer coats. Careful examination of different particles will detect some which consist of the elongated vertical exterior cells, containing resin, while others are the shrunken parenchyma cells of the second layer, whose structure is indistinct.

Flückiger calls the first layer yellow, which hardly seems correct, as the appearance is nearly black. It is unnecessary, however, to attempt a minute study of these cells, as one is only required to be able to recognize their appearance and in addition to know something of the relative proportion of ground pepper which they should form as they are added in excess as pepper dust, the waste hulls of pepper being often used as an adulterant. The colored portion of a ground black pepper it will be found divides itself into two classes, the dark particles which have just been mentioned and the deep reddish ones, which are made up of the testa of the seed and its adherent parenchyma. The two will be readily recognized and distinguished from adulterants by the investigator.

The differences in the appearance of the peppers from various sources is sufficiently marked to be readily noticed when samples of each are placed side by side, but otherwise it is almost impossible to identify them. The best method of judging their quality and the one in use in the trade is by weight. Malabar is considered the heaviest. Blyth gives the following figures:

100 peppercorns of—	Grams.
Penang	6.2496
Malabar	6.0536
Sumatra	5.1476
Trevy	4.5736
Tellicherry	4.5076

Tellicherry is the Malabar or West Coast port, so that variations must occur, as would be natural, in different samples.

We have found some samples to weigh—

Serial No.	Source.	Weight per 100 grams.	Percentage of dust and dirt.
	Black.		
4514	Unknown	5.9000	
4840	Unknown	5.4600	
4894	Acheen	4.525	2.5
4895	West Coast	5.085	4.3
4896	Singapore	4.870	8.3
	White.		
4516	Unknown	5.1300	
4898	Singapore	4.9600	1.4

The white pepper is of course the cleaner.

ADULTERANTS.

The common adulterants to be found in peppers are said to be flours or starches of cereals and potatoes, sago, mustard husk, linseed and capsicum, pepper dust, sawdust, gypsum, and other odds and ends.

Of the adulterations of pepper Blyth enumerates many, among them the celebrated pepper dusts designated as "P. D.", "H. P. D.," and "W. P. D.," and known as pepper dust, composed of linseed cake; hot-pepper dust, composed of mustard husks chiefly, and white-pepper dust, composed of ground rice. In this country the use of ground corn or rice, mustard hulls, cocoanut shells, and other similar refuse is very common, but whether they have been derived from goods sold as H. P. D. and W. P. D." we were unable to ascertain. Other refuse is also frequently found in cheap peppers, but sand does not seem to be as often added here as abroad. We have found the white peppers much freer from adulteration than the black. It is learned from Dr. Ellis, of Toronto, that roasted cocoanut shells are in common use now as an adulterant of all spices, and are of course easily introduced into peppers. They have not been found in the specimens which we have examined. Pepper husks, mustard hulls, yellow corn, cracker dust, charcoal, and mineral matter have been detected by their characteristic appearances. The presence of pepper husks and charcoal is generally known by the immensely increased proportion of black particles in the field, as appears in Fig. 43, Plate XVII. A careful sorting of the coarser particles under a low power of the dissecting microscope and selection, for example, of the shining white grains of rice or yellow particles of corn from the more oily pepper cells, enables us to examine the starches separately with plain and polarized light. The appearance of the true pepper powder and one in which rice starch is present is given in Plate XXII, Figs. 43 and 44. Pepper starch is so much smaller than any other which we meet with, that it is not easily confused with it. Fig. 65, Plate XXVIII, gives an idea of its size as compared with others. With the dissecting microscope it is also convenient to go over the pepper powder and pick out any other class of suspicious particles for examination with higher power. With a little practice it soon becomes easy to tell an adulterated specimen even with a cursory examination with a lower power or a hand lens. In this way, in our experience, one or two foreign substances have been found which have not been identified, but which were evidently parts of the husks or coverings of some seed or fruit. The shell of the cocoanut, as has been said, has not been met with as an adulterant, but it is not at all difficult to identify, as its structure, with its innumerable stone cells and fibrous tissue, is very characteristic after treatment with Schulze's reagent.

The microscopic examination thus gives very certain indications of the quality of peppers, although frequently the eye without aid will detect a fictitious appearance. The chemical examination, on the other hand, as will be shown, serves as a reliable means of confirmation in many instances, and gives evidence of the quantity as well as kind of the adulteration. A considerable amount of information has been accumulated in regard to the proximate composition of peppers. Flückiger quotes authorities for the statement that black pepper contains from 1.6 to 2.2 per cent. of volatile oil, of the character of a terpene and optically active; also a nitrogenous substance known as piperine to the extent of 2 to 8 per cent. Husemann and Hilger* give reference to papers by several investigators (see bibliography), and describes piperine as soluble in alcohol, and less so in ether. This substance, which is characteristic, will be found, therefore, in the ether extract of the spice, together with the volatile oil.

Blyth has made an examination of several peppers, and gives results which are useful for reference.

* Die Pflanzenstoffe, B. 2. S. 486.

Analysis of ash of Tellicherry pepper.

	Per cent.
Potash	24.38
Soda	3.23
Magnesia	13.00
Lime	11.60
Iron	.30
Phosphoric acid	8.47
Sulphuric acid	9.61
Chlorine	7.57
Carbonic acid	14.00
Sand	6.53

The sand, he finds, the most variable constituent, but never above 9 per cent. of the ash except in cases of willful adulteration. Phosphoric acid averages 8.5 per cent. of the ash, which is considered characteristic. He has also identified nitrates in peppers, finding in—

	Per cent.
Penang	.04470
Malabar	.03858
Tellicherry	.08800
Sumatra	.06360
Trang	.11870

The average proximate composition he finds to be—

	Per cent.
Volatile oil	1.04
Acrid resin	1.77
Piperine	5.17
Substances soluble in water, gum, starch, and other matters substracting ash	14.74
Substances insoluble in alcohol and water	67.75
Water	9.53
	100.00

Following are some analyses made by Blyth in 1876:

	Hygroscopic moisture.	Piperine in pepper, dried at 100°.	Resin in pepper, dried at 100°.	Aqueous extract in pepper, dried at 100°.	Ash in pepper, dried at 100°.	
					Soluble in water.	Total.
Penang	9.53	5.57	2.08	18.33	2.21	4.18
Tellicherry	12.90	4.68	1.70	16.50	3.38	5.77
Sumatra	10.10	4.70	1.74	17.59	2.62	4.31
Malabar	10.54	4.63	1.74	20.37	3.45	5.19
Trang	11.66	4.60	1.70	18.17	2.53	4.77
White pepper (com.)	10.30	5.60	2.05	......	.56	1.12
Long pepper	......	1.80	.80	16.82	4.47	8.30

The process for the estimation of piperine approved by Blyth is extraction with petroleum ether and treatment of the extract with sodic hydrate to remove the resin. Subsequent investigations by Lenz condemn this method, however.

More recently Rottger* has investigated the pepper-corn with especial consideration of the question of detection of adulteration, and decided that the examination of commercial peppers should be directed to determinations of the inorganic constituents, the percentage of water, and the microscope, with determinations of the soluble and insoluble ash and piperine in certain instances. He decides that the alcohol and ether extracts are of no value, quoting great variations in his results and those of others. He found—

	For ether extract, indirectly determined.	For alcohol extract of 90 per cent.
	Per cent.	*Per cent.*
White pepper	8.0 to 10.7	10.0 to 11.8
Black pepper	7.9 12.1	12.3 16.7

Borgman, Wolff, and Biechele† likewise have determined the amount of alcohol extract, but have neglected the ether extract. It seems difficult to understand why the alcohol extract should be selected, as the ether is much simpler, and refers almost directly to the amount of volatile oil and piperine which the spice contains, without so much of the indefinite resin and sugar which the alcohol extracts. The determination of water was made as follows by Rottger: The powdered pepper was placed for three hours over sulphuric acid, and a portion then weighed out and dried at 100° C. for one and a half hours, then for a quarter of an hour at a time until it begins to gain weight. He found the variations to be between 12.6 and 14.7 for black pepper, and 12.9 and and 14.5 for white pepper.

This striking agreement, he considers, makes this determination of value. It is open to serious criticism and is of little value, in our view, for the following reason: By consulting our investigations on the hygroscopic character of organic matter in a state of fine division,‡ it will be seen that allowing peppers to remain over sulphuric acid for three hours would not accomplish the end desired, at least in our climate, viz, reducing the moisture in all to a constant figure, and in addition Rottger takes no account of the volatile oil lost at 100°. In our analyses we find, in fact, much less water than he does, as is usual in all organic material in our drier climate, and no greater variation among the peppers than the adulterated specimens. Practical tests of the method also proved unsatisfactory.

* Ber. uber d. 4 Ver. Bayrisch. Vertreter der angew Chemie, 97-102.

† Vide Bibliography.

‡ Bull. No. 4, Div. of Chem., Department of Agriculture.

The per cent. of ash Rottger finds for black pepper to be between 3.4 and 5.1 per cent., white pepper between .8 and 2.9 per cent., with an exception in the case of Lampong pepper, which has 6.4 per cent. He concludes, with other investigators, that 6 is the highest allowable figure for ash in black pepper, with anything above 5 as suspicious. Three per cent. is, in the same way, the highest allowable figure for white pepper.

Of the composition of the ash he says:

The facts point to the conclusion that an exhaustive investigation of the mineral constituents in many cases may be of benefit in forming an opinion of the quality and purity of peppers.*

He found the following extremes:

	Black.		White.	
Fe_2O_3		2.2		
Mn_2O_3		.89		
K_2O	27.4 to	34.7	5.1 to	7.1
Cl	3.6	8.7	.5	.9
SiO_2	1.5	6.3	1.0	2.6
P_2O_5, water sol	.11	.91	....	....
P_2O_5, insol	8.2	12.5	30.8	30.7

He gives the following detailed analyses:

Percentage composition of the pepper ash.

	Black pepper.			White pepper.	
	Unknown origin.		Malabar, 1883.	Unknown origin.	Singapore.
SiO_2	6.36 to	1.61	1.54	2.62	1.46
HCl	5.59	6.83	8.71	.58	.90
SO_3	4.03	4.95	4.00	3.24	3.75
CO_2	17.28	20.10	19.17	11.90	10.01
P_2O_5	11.10	9.46	11.06	29.34	30.75
K_2O	32.49	34.72	27.39	5.10	7.15
Na_2O	1.55	4.77	5.50	.74	.84
CaO	16.07	13.53	15.02	35.12	31.05
MgO	3.31	4.46	7.56	9.54	11.64
Fe_2O_3	2.16	.99	.85	2.22	1.86
Mn_2O_3	.81		.18	.80	.21

Rottger then discusses the determination of the piperine, and allows that for simplicity and accuracy drying the powder with milk of lime and extraction with ether is to be preferred. When the ether is pure, dry, and free from alcohol we find lime is of little use, or rather a complication, and that for purposes of detecting adulteration the ether extract alone furnishes all the information desired.

Lenz† has determined the amount of sugar produced by inverting the starch in fourteen peppers, and in the common adulterants, with acid. He found all the samples gave an equivalent of more than 50 per cent.

* Halenke has more recently discussed this subject: vide bibliography, Appendix A.

† Zeit. Anal. Chem., 1884, **23**, 501.

of sugar on the ash free organic matter of the pepper, while all the adulterants gave less than 30 per cent., with the exception of those which are starchy, as flours and meals.

Rottger repeated this determination, showing that some other substances besides starch were inverted by the acid, and obtained the following results:

Black pepper sugar equivalent	57.2 to 60.3
White pepper sugar equivalent	59.6 to 74.4

The Lampong pepper gave only 41.70. Such great variations he considers fatal to the method as a means of detecting adulterations. His conclusions seem not entirely justified, as a review of Lenz's figures will show.

Lenz in his paper affirms that any extract determination is useless, as with various adulterants the results may be very close to actual pepper. Petroleum ether he shows to be unreliable, the amount of extract depending on the kind of extraction apparatus used. There certainly should be no difficulty of purely manipulative detail of this description, for if sufficient time is given the solvent will work the same under all conditions, but not less than twenty hours' continuous extraction should be allowed, and it is not fair to generalize on an analysis where the extraction was continued less than that time, the poor results being due only to a probable faultily manner of manipulation, as we have met with no such trouble.

Lenz's conclusions seem hardly just, and while there may be cases where adulterants would not be detected by an extract determination, in the majority it is a great assistance. Lenz also refers to the method of separation of the powdered particles of pepper adulterants by means of liquids of certain specific gravities, and pronounces it unsuitable. He prefers the treatment with iodine solution and the selection of the particles not blued for examination under the microscope as adulterants. We have found it perfectly simple and desirable to use the method of separation with sieves, and to examine the coarse powder, with or without treatment, under the microscope, when, with a little experience, it is easy to distinguish and recognize the source of particles not pepper after a careful examination with high powers.

He also casts doubt upon the value of an ash determination, and owing to the great variations which he finds quoted as possible, recommends calculating all results on an ash free basis. He, however, admits that a carefully and properly cleaned pepper-corn will not usually contain more than 6 per cent., and his strictures, therefore, do not seem to be consistent. He places reliance only on the process of his own invention, determinations of sugar corresponding to the starch and other invertible substances, with supplementary determinations of water and ash and microscopic examination. His results were as follows:

List of equivalent percentage of reducing sugars in ash free organic substance of peppers and adulterants.

No.	Name.	Ash.	Dry residue.	Ash free dry residue.	Sugar equivalent in sample.	Sugar equivalent in ash free dry sample.	Remarks.
1	Black Batavia pepper	3.85	87.68	83.83	43.8	52.3	Inverted directly.
2	Long pepper (2)	8.68	88.77	80.12	44.2	55.2	Inverted after extraction with water.
3	Black Singapore	3.62	86.88	83.26	43.9	52.8	Inverted directly.
4	Do	3.62	86.88	83.26	45.0	54.1	Inverted after extraction with alcohol.
5	Do	3.62	86.88	83.26	44.1	53.0	After water.
6	White pepper	.99	87.50	86.60	51.8	59.9	Do.
7	Palm-cake meal (1)	3.71	89.76	86.05	22.7	26.4	After water and alcohol.
8	Do	3.71	89.76	86.05	19.1	22.2	After water.
9	Do	3.71	89.76	86.05	22.7	26.4	Direct.
10	Palm-cake meal (2)	3.65	89.35	85.70	{22.4 22.5	26.1 26.2	} Do.
11	Do	3.65	89.35	85.70	19.7	23.0	After water.
12	Palm-cake meal (3)	3.54	89.88	86.34	19.4	22.5	Do.
13	Palm-cake, pure	1.89	93.44	91.55	11.1	12.1	After ether and alcohol.
14	Pepper husks	15.61	89.50	73.89	11.5	15.6	After water.
15	Pepper husks picked out of commercial pepper.	9.21	88.64	79.43	13.0	16.4	Do.
16	Commercial pepper husks.	20.29	88.42	68.13	11.5	16.9	Do.
17	Commercial pepper powder containing palm-cake meal.	5.15	88.76	83.55	35.9	43.0	Do.
18	Pepper (3), with 28 per cent. of palm-cake meal (3).	3.59	87.88	84.29	36.0	42.7	Do.
19	Same with 42.4 per cent.	3.58	88.38	84.80	33.7	39.7	Do.
20	Walnut shells	1.04	89.34	88.30	17.7	20.0	Do.
21	Buckwheat meal	2.10	86.58	84.48	56.1	66.4	Direct.
22	Dried and roasted bread.	1.15	100.00	98.85	....	86.3	Do.
23	Do	1.15	100.00	98.85	....	62.6	After water.

Lenz's method of inverting was this: 3 to 4 grams of the substance to be examined was treated for three to four hours in a flask with 250 c.c. of water, being repeatedly shaken. It was then filtered off, washed with water, and the moist powder washed back into the flask, and to 200 c.c. of water 25 c.c. of 25 per cent. hydrochloric acid added. The flask was provided with a cork and tube one meter long and placed in a bath of boiling water and kept there three hours, with shaking. It is then made up on cooling to 500 c.c., after careful neutralization with soda. This liquid was then titrated with Fehling solution. When palm-cake was present it was found necessary to add a little zinc chloride to clear the solution. Most of the surrogates for pepper used in Germany Lenz found to be free from starch, so that this method would seem to be of wide applicability. He remarks, however, that other substances besides starch may be inverted, and for this reason it is necessary to adhere closely to one method of working. We shall from our own experience and that of others learn more in regard to the capabilities and usefulness of this method.

Haslinger and Moslinger* have also published some observations on pepper and its adulteration which are of interest. They show that in Germany the addition of grains of paradise, the seed of *Amomum Melegueta*, is a common practice whose detection can be accomplished most readily with the microscope, after a study of the structure of the grains of paradise, which is very characteristic. The starch cells are larger than in pepper, 3 to 6 times as long as hard, but the starch itself is scarcely distinguishable. The cells are arranged in parallel lines forming bundles pointed at the end. The cells remain white when treated with hydrochloric acid, while those of pepper are yellower.

These writers also looked into the ash of commercial samples of pepper and found from 4.1 to 27.0 per cent. of inorganic substance insoluble in hydrochloric acid where in peppers ground by themselves only .3 and .8 per cent. occurred. They also found pepper siftings, pepper husks, and other refuse in use as adulterants and followed up Lenz's suggestions as to determination of reducing sugar produced from the samples by acid, by examining pure pepper corns ground by themselves, and also pepper husks, and extending the determinations to cellulose also. The "dextrose," as they denominate it, was determined according to Allihn, the "cellulose" according to Heuberger. The results were as follows:

	Dextrose.	Cellulose.
Black pepper, pure	56.0	15.6
Pepper husks, pure	16.4	45.0
Four samples for investigation:		
I	46.4	23.4
II	40.8	28.1
III	44.9	23.3
IV	41.5	26.8
Pepper siftings	21.6	37.4

From these figures they give the following formulæ for calculating adulterations where:

x=per cent. of pure pepper.

y=per cent. of hulls.

s=per cent. of dextrose or cellulose in sample.

a=per cent. of dextrose in pure pepper.

b=per cent. of dextrose in husks.

For the dextrose figures:

$$x=\frac{100s-1640}{39.6}$$

For the cellulose figures:

$$x=\frac{4500-100s}{29.35}$$

* Ber. 1. Ver. Bay. Verterter ang. Chemie, 101-110.

Calculated on this basis the four samples were found to consist of:

	Pure pepper husks and pepper.			
	On the ground of dextrose det.		On ground of cellulose det.	
I	75.8 and	24.2	73.5 and	26.5
II	61.6	38.4	37.5	42.5
III	72.1	27.9	74.0	26.0
IV	63.3	36.7	65.4	34.6

These figures show a fair agreement, and, in the opinion of the authors, entitle the method to consideration. They condemn, however, severely placing any reliance on determinations of the alcohol extract.

Weigmann* has also examined a number of pure peppers, and obtained results which do not harmonize with those of Lenz. He finds:

	White.	Black.
Ash	1.0 to 3.0	3.0 to 7.0
Starch (Lenz method)	53.0 63.0	32.0 44.0
Fiber	5.0 6.0	12.0 15.0
Water	12.0 to 15.0	

Our experience with the inversion of starch by acids is such as to make it seem very probable that, without the necessary attention to details, it would be very possible to obtain such results as those last given from lack of complete conversion of starch to reducing sugar or the inversion of other substances, and in the discussion of our analyses this will be referred to.

In the second report† of the Laboratoire Municipal de Paris the subject of pepper and its adulteration as practiced in France is discussed. There whole peppers are made artificially from plaster, gum, and a little pepper, and the ground article with the most diverse substances, such as hemp-seed cake, colza, rape and beechnut cakes, starches, residues from the manufacture of potato starch, mineral matter, sweeping of spice warehouses sold as pepper dust, and so forth. The residue from the manufacture of potato starch has, after fermentation, a pungent taste which makes it a desirable adulterant, but the most common one is the powdered kernel of the olive, which is yellowish white in color and possesses all the outward characteristics of white pepper and gives practically the same amount of ash. To give this powder the proper taste and pungency there was added Cayenne, powdered bay leaves, and dried and powdered orange skins. The mixture is recognized without difficulty by chemical and microscopic examination, the latter of which gives an absolute proof of the character of the substance.

It is recommended to separate the olive kernels from pepper by the use of a mixture of glycerine and water of a Sp. Gr. of 1.173 at 10° C., in which the former sink. After decantation they can be examined

* Rep. anal. Chem. **6**, 399-40.

† Documents sur les falsifications des Matieres alimentaires, Paris, 1885, p. 688-695.

microscopically. The structure is that characteristic of the hard thickened schlerenchyma or stone cells, polyhedral and elongated in shape with thickened walls and little filiform canals. They are most readily made out with polarized light, toward which they are optically active, while the remaining particles of pepper or pepper husks are not seen in the dark field, being inactive.

Of this adulterant H. Rabourdin has made some investigations, publishing his results in an interesting paper,* giving a general account of the various peppers of commerce and the use of olive stones as an adulterant, as well as other materials already mentioned. He finds no difficulty in recognizing the falsification owing to the presence of the numerous sclerenchyma or stone cells, which are distinguished readily with polarized light, but the quantitative determination is more difficult. This, however, he affirms, can be accomplished by determining the residue left on boiling the suspected sample for one hour with 1 per cent. sulphuric acid after thorough washing with water. In the course of the operation the presence of the olive stones is apparent from their clinging in the form of a reddish powder to the walls of the flask or beaker in which the digestion has taken place, and separating more or less from the pepper hulls on account of their different specific gravity.

For pure peppers the following percentage of residue was found:

	Per cent.	Mean.
Tellicherry	30.3 to 27.8	29.4
Alepy	31.5 31.8	31.7
Saigon	28.7 29.2	29.0
Singapore	33.2 34.0	33.7
Penang	33.8 34.2	34.0
Sumatra	33.0	......
Java	37.5 37.7	37.6
White, pure	17.5	17.5
Powdered, pure	29.2 29.0	......
Do	30.5 35.5	......

On the other hand olive stones were found to contain:

	Per cent.	Mean.
Coarse gray	74.2 to 75.0	74.6
Fine gray	74.2 74.6	74.4
Coarse white	74.5	......
Fine white	74.5	......
Pepper dust	65.5	......

From these figures the following factors are derived:

	Per cent.
White pepper	17.5
Malabar, Tellicherry, and Saigon	30.0
Alepy	32.0
Others known as light peppers	35.0
Olive stones	74.5
Pepper refuse	75.5

*J. de Pharm. et de Chimie, [5], 9, 289-297.

And if y is the per cent. of residue, a the per cent. in pure pepper, b the per cent. in olive stones, the amount of addition can be calculated from the following equations:

$$x+y=100 \qquad ax+by=p$$

$$y=\frac{p-a}{b-a}$$

where b can be replaced by 74.5 or 65.5 as the case may be.

Working in this way 10 ground peppers, guaranteed pure, were found to contain from 40 to 60 per cent. of olive stones, and these contained "P.D." to the extent of 14 to 20 per cent.

Control experiments with known mixtures seem to have been satisfactory.

The same author also extended his experiments to a comparison of the properties and separation of the cellulose derived from a mixture of pepper and olive stones, depending upon the difference in specific gravity, with results which can be found in his original paper.

The residues of starch factories always contain enough starch grains to make their identification easy.

Very recently Chas. Heisch* has given in the Analyst his experience in the examination of peppers, to see if there were any reliable mode of judging of the amount of adulterants in adulterated samples except by determinations of ash which give no indication of added organic matter. He also endeavored to find if it were possible to cleanse pepper corns so that the ash should be free from sand. Assisted by a large buyer and grinders of pepper he found that as the result of the grinder's experience no ground pepper should be sent to market which contains over 6 per cent. of total ash. In this respect they agree with the Bavarian chemists. He also placed some faith in the determination of starch and calculated, as did Lenz, his results on dry ash free organic matter.

The starch was estimated "by boiling the finely ground pepper for three hours with 10 per cent. hydrochloric acid, and taking the rotation in the resulting liquid." He endeavored to check his results by determining that there was insufficient "gum or other matters to affect the rotatory power" but neglects to see how much of the substances allied to cellulose are converted into optically active substances which would probably be important. Stating the results, however, as reducing sugar equivalent to pepper with Lenz, the error becomes of slight importance.

The determination of piperine was rough, and the results seemed of little service.

*Analyst, 2, 186–190, October, 1886.

The results were as follows:

No.	Name of sample.	Water.	Ash of dry pepper. Total.	Soluble in H_2O.	Soluble in HCl.	Insoluble.	Alkalinity as K_2O.	On ash and water free pepper. Starch.	Alcohol extract.	Piperine.
	Black Pepper:									
1	Acheen Penang	9.46	8.90	1.54	3.07	4.38	.72	48.53	12.26	6.04
2	Trang	9.22	8.85	1.60	3.83	3.42	.81	54.06	12.28	4.05
3	Singapore	14.36	5.41	2.07	2.52	.82	.91	56.24	12.41	7.14
4	Tellicherry	13.76	5.28	3.34	1.90	.04	1.41	56.67	12.67	6.88
5	Penang	12.98	6.45	3.10	2.44	.91	1.19	51.06	16.20	9.38
6	Tellicherry (brushed)	13.01	6.41	2.38	2.84	1.20	1.57	55.87	13.62	7.86
7	Gray light dusty Singapore	13.94	5.39	2.48	2.18	.73	1.09	54.93	11.62	6.30
8	Good B, Singapore	14.10	4.35	2.48	1.51	.36	1.14	54.54	10.47	6.06
	White Pepper:									
9	Penang	15.86	3.78	0.62	2.80	.36	.22	77.68	9.73	5.54
10	Singapore	17.32	1.28	.22	0.85	.22	.00	76.35	9.49	6.14
11	Siam	13.67	1.81	.25	.92	.69	.11	76.27	9.23	5.13
	As ground for market:									
12	Fine white	13.90	1.58	.16	.90	.52	.00	75.31	10.60	4.51
13	Finest	14.13	2.18	.50	1.50	.17	.11	84.69	9.53	4.70
14	I super	14.40	1.41	.37	1.03	.00	.11	85.26	9.63	4.90
	Long pepper:									
15	No. 1, H	12.15	13.48	2.28	5.52	5.68	.53	58.98	8.29	1.71
16	No. 2, T	14.93	11.98	2.37	5.83	3.69	.82	46.16	8.52	1.70
17	Black pepper husks	12.37	11.90	2.12	6.37	3.41	.48	41.71	13.81	4.84
18	Do., with same whole	12.60	9.04	3.00	4.12	1.92	.02	47.36	13.07	4.10
19	Sifting before grinding	7.96	51.39	1.02	6.47	43.90	.80	30.66	7.52	1.15
20	Black pepper, for sale of which fine was inflicted	11.12	14.70	2.02	4.07	8.61	.80	35.85	11.57	2.02
21	Poivrette used to mix with pepper	8.52	3.85	.96	1.05	1.84	0.21	0.00	2.31	.....
22	10 per cent. poivrette, 90 per cent. No. 4	13.34	5.04	2.88	1.78	.38	1.14	49.98	.....	.....
23	30 per cent. rice, 70 per cent. No. 4	12.76	3.10	1.68	1.39	.03	.89	88.21	.....	.....

Of the above samples Nos. 1 to 5 and 7 to 8 were black pepper corns ground just as imported. The uniformity in the starch in all these lead Heisch to believe that any result under 50 per cent. should be regarded as suspicious, it being very easy to detect the addition of foreign starch, such as rice. Of the white peppers the first three are white pepper corns ground as imported, the next three black corns decorticated in England and then ground.

Of the long pepper Heisch says the starch is double the size of the ordinary and much more angular and like rice. Care must be taken therefore not to confound them. The poivrette is made from olive stones.

The figures are of interest and would seem to confirm the work of Lenz.

Prof. J. Campbell Brown has devoted much time to the subject of pepper and has very recently called attention in England to an adulterant which first made its appearance in Liverpool last summer and since then has been often met with. It is known as pepperette or poivrette, and proves to be the same adulterant so often mentioned in France, olive stones. It resembled walnut shells and almond shells somewhat, but olive stones more so.

Brown gives the following analyses and says:*

	Ash.	Matters soluble by boiling in diluted acid.	Albuminous and other matters soluble in alkali.	Woody fiber, insoluble in acid and alkali.	Starch.
White pepperette	1.33	38.32	14.08	48.48	None.
Black pepperette	2.47	34.55	17.66	47.69	None.
Ground almond shells	2.05	23.53	24.79	51.68	None.
Ground olive stones	1.61	39.08	15.04	45.38	None.

The stones of olives, imported in pickle for table use, gave 3.68 per cent. of ash, but well-washed olive-stones, thoroughly burnt to a white ash, gave under 2 per cent. of ash-like poivrette. "White poivrette" is therefore cleaned very pale, and perhaps partly bleached olive-stones or precisely similar tissue; black poivrette is the same, mixed with a little black husk. It is to be noted that although it contains no starch, yet it yields some sugar to Fehling's solution, after being boiled for some time with dilute hydrochloric acid. The quantity depends on the length of time and strength of acid, but may be stated approximately about 10 per cent. It is important to bear this fact in mind when making a full chemical analysis of pepper containing poivrette. After removing from such a mixture the matters soluble by boiling in dilute caustic alkali, the woody fiber which remains has a yellow color. It consists of the poivrette and some of the cells of pepper husk and one of the subcortical layers of the pepper berry. The pepper cells are made lighter and the poivrette cells darker by the alkali, so that the two are more nearly of a similar yellow color after treatment with alkali. This renders it more difficult to distinguish such of the cells as have somewhat similar markings, but it enables us to distinguish more clearly as poivrette the many torn particles which have no definite form or markings. The final examination of the complete cells is better made with good daylight rather than with artificial light, and in a portion which has been treated with water only.

The pepper cells are mostly different in shape and are colored, and have generally a dark substance in the interior. They are not numerous, but the quantity varies in commercial samples, owing to the modern practice of decorticating the pepper berry to every different extent possible, and mixing the various portions so obtained, including husks, in every variety of proportion with each other or with ordinary pepper. Each individual analyst must make himself familiar with both kinds of cells, as no description can convey an adequate idea of either. In order to form a judgment regarding the proportions of the different chemical constituents of commercial samples, we require to know the chemical composition of the different layers of the pepper-corn, and I hope soon to communicate to the society some figures bearing on this point, as well as to notice some other substances used in the sophistication of pepper.

It is interesting to note that the exemption, mentioned in section 8 of the sale of food and drugs act, in the case of a label being affixed to the article sold intimating that the same is a mixture, does not apply in the case of poivrette, the admixture being made manifestly for the purpose of fraudulently increasing the weight and bulk.

In a subsequent note Brown † warns analysts not to confuse an excessive amount of cortical cells of the pepper husk for poivrette, as they are somewhat similar. This, however, would certainly not occur if authentic samples of pepper and olive-stones were used for comparison.

Brown also contributes a paper to the Analyst § on the use of "long pepper," *Chavica Roxburghii*, as an admixture to the ordinary ground

* Analyst, **12**, 23–25.
† Analyst, **12**, 47–48.
§ Analyst, **12**, 67–70.

article, showing that it should be discouraged, from the fact that . brings with it a large amount of dirt and mineral matter, and has a disagreeable offensive odor developed by warmth. Brown says:

It is now time that all should take up a decided position in regard to this form of adulteration. Long pepper is the fruit of *Charica Roxburghii*,* and does not consist merely of the berries analogous to the pepper-corns of the true pepper-plant; it bears much the same relation to them that wild grass-seed would bear to oatmeal. It consists of the small berries with the husks and indurated coverings hardened together and to the central woody stem, much in the same way that in pines the seed and coverings are all hardened into one cone. Long pepper is for the most part derived from wild plants of *Charica Roxburghii*, which grow by the sides of the water-courses in India. Consequently it always brings with it a mass of dirt, picked up from the soil of the banks whereon it grows, embedded in the crevices and irregularities of the fruit, which dirt the native collector takes care not to lessen, but rather to increase, seeing that he is paid by weight for what he brings down to the merchants.

In commerce we find accordingly that it has always from 3 to 7 per cent. of insoluble sand and clay, in addition to the proper ash of the fruit. And it is difficult, if not impossible, to clean long pepper before grinding in the way that true pepper can easily be cleaned; it can with difficulty be cleaned by hand.

The ash contains a very large proportion of salts insoluble in hydrochloric acid. When ground, the hard husk and woody center, as well as the dirt, are necessarily ground along with the minute berries. The ground long pepper contains not only sand, but more woody fibre than ground genuine pepper of the corresponding shade, although not so much total cellulose as the most husky black pepper. It has the composition shown by Mr. Heisch in his paper. I can confirm his results by the following:

Analyses of long pepper carefully cleaned by hand.

	Total a	Sand and ash insoluble in HCl.	Total matter soluble in 10 per cent. HCl.	Starch and matters convertible into sugar.	Albuminous matter soluble in alkali.	Cellulose.	Extracted by alcohol.	Extracted by ether.	Total nitrogen.
1	8.91	1.2	67.83	44.04	15.47	15.70	7.7	5.5	2.1
2	8.98	1.1	68.31	49.34	17.42	10.50	7.6	4.9	2.0
3	9.61	1.5	65.91	44.61	15.51	10.73	10.5	8.6	2.3

Although the cost of long pepper is at present nearly as high as some very inferior varieties of black pepper, yet the price is generally decidedly lower; even now long pepper is much cheaper than the pepper with which it has been sometimes mixed of late, and its use affords a handsome illegitimate profit, to the detriment both of the grocer and his customer. Long pepper has been, and is, legitimately used for pickles, but it is not known, nor has it been recognized by the trade, as ground long pepper; and all the respectable grocers, and others of whom I have inquired, say decidedly that they would not buy, nor retain, if received, any ground pepper which they knew or suspected to contain an admixture of long pepper. In fact, it is no more right to give pepper containing long pepper in response to a request for simply "pepper" than it would be to give horse-chestnuts instead of Spanish chestnuts in response to a request for simply "chestnuts." It may, of course, be sold as ground long pepper without offense, but no one would buy it. Not only is long pepper a fraudulent admixture in ground pepper, but it is objectionable on the score of quality and flavor. Its disagreeable, offensive odor is developed by warmth. Any candid person can convince himself of the real cause of the objections which housekeepers and grocers alike have to ground long pepper if he will heat up a piece of cold meat between two plates and sprinkle some fresh long pepper on it; the smell and flavor are so offensive that he will feel obliged to reject the meat.

Much of that which one gets whole in shops is very old, and has lost much of its flavor and strength, so small a sale does it command.

The presence of long pepper in ground pepper may be determined by the following characters:

1. *Color.*—If any serious quantity of long pepper is ground in with the ordinary pepper it imparts some of its peculiar slaty color; but this is made much lighter by the now very common practice of sifting out much of the darker or husky portions of the long pepper before mixing it with the genuine pepper. Bleaching is also resorted to, but not hitherto very effectively.

2. The odor of the mixture when warmed is unmistakable by an educated olfactory sense, even if the quantity is comparatively moderate. Attempts are made to disguise the odor by bleaching, but this has not been successful. The ethereal extract also, and even the alcohol extract from which the solvent has been evaporated at a low temperature, yields, when warmed, the characteristic odor very plainly.

3. Long pepper introduces sand into the pepper with which it is mixed, often to a considerable amount. If the pepper is white, this has more importance than has hitherto been accorded to it; for white pepper does not contain, even as imported, 2½ per cent. of sand, and any white pepper containing so much sand must have had the sand improperly introduced, either by direct mixing of Calais sand or in some other way.

Long pepper from which the husk particles have been sifted out when added to white pepper invariably introduces its sand along with it, as well as some spent bleach, if attempts have been made to bleach it.

4. The woody matter in ground long pepper is always considerable, arising both from the smallness of the berries, compared with the hardened setting, and from the central woody tube. This may be detected either by chemical analysis or by the microscope, and some of it by the naked eye or a large hand lens.

If the sample is spread out in a smooth thin layer on strong paper, by means of an ivory paper-knife, pieces of fluffy woody fiber will be detected, especially if the smooth thin layer be tapped lightly from below. Those pieces come from the central part of the indurated catkin which cannot be completely ground fine as genuine pepper stalks are, and are very characteristic if carefully examined. Much of these are of course removed by the grinders' sieves, but enough finds its way through the meshes of the silk to be useful as a corroborative indication.

5. Particles of husks, if present, can be distinguished from genuine pepper husks.

6. A proportion of the starch granules of long pepper are of larger size, above .0002 inch, and of angular shape, very slightly smaller than rice granules, and more loosely aggregated in clusters or isolated.

Brown also calls attention to the statement of authorities that genuine pepper starch is round in form, and shows that this is not always the case. By reference to our illustration, Fig. 65, Plate XXVIII, it will be seen that he is correct. He has lately found* that Dhoura corn, a variety of sorghum, is being largely used in England as a diluent of pepper. The grain is well known in this country as Egyptian corn, and is a common crop in the South and Southwest, but has not been used here as an adulterant. Brown says:

I have met with it only about four times in pepper, but it probably occurs more frequently in other districts. It is known in England as great millet or Turkish

* Analyst, **12**, 89-90.

millet, and is the grain (with an integument, but without the husk) of one of the cereal grasses, *Sorghum vulgare*.

It is a roundish or oval somewhat flattened grain, size from one-eighth to one-fifth of an inch in diameter, white in color and brittle, with a thin, smooth integument or testa, showing under a high microscopic power, on the inner surface, an aggregation of very small granules, which become blue by iodine. The body of the seed is very white, and consists mainly of roundish or irregular starch granules, varying in size from .0001 up to .0006 of an inch in diameter, and showing under polarized light a nearly right-angled cross; and of larger irregularly rounded granules of starch from .0005 up to .0013 of an inch in diameter, showing no cross, or only a very faint one, under polarized light.

Some of the first-named granules have a hilum and star in the centre, somewhat like bean starch. By boiling with caustic alkali the cellular membrane which binds the starch granules together is disclosed.

The influence of an admixture of sorghum with pepper upon analysis of the latter will be seen from the following analysis of sorghum grains:

Moisture 11 per cent.

Composition of the dried sample.

	I.	II.
Ash	1.31	1.69
Soluble in 10 per cent. hydrochloric acid	90.70	87.80
Starch	75.20	73.00
Albuminous matters soluble in caustic alkali	6.71	7.96
Cellulose	2.56	4.19
Alcoholic extract	10.36	7.96
Ethereal extract	10.40	7.30
Nitrogen	1.82	1.79

There would be no difficulty in detecting it.

Although as yet these substances do not seem to have reached us as far as the samples which we have examined show they must be carefully watched for.

In this country considerable has been published as to the adulterations of pepper, but little in regard to the manner of detecting them. We have already spoken of the large numbers of samples which have been examined in different years by the public analysts of Canada and smaller numbers by those of Massachusetts and New York. Reference to the reports of the department of inland revenue of the Dominion (supplements on adulteration of food) shows that wheat flour, husks, cayenne, cocoanut shells, and pepper dust, milling refuse, pea meal, and sand and clay are in very common use. In the United States the samples examined have apparently proved no better, for while in Canada in 1885 twenty-nine out of sixty samples were adulterated mostly from 10 to 20 per cent., but reaching 75 per cent.; in New York in 1882, out of forty-seven, thirty-three were adulterated, and in Massachusetts in 1884 Wood found one hundred and four in one hundred and ninety-nine impure, and in 1883 69 to 70 per cent. were bad.

We are thus supplied with considerable experience in the examination of peppers, the results of which furnish the basis of a scheme for general use. Thus in examining a sample I should propose to proceed as follows:

METHOD OF EXAMINING PEPPERS MICROSCOPICALLY.

As a preliminary the sieve examination, already mentioned, is of value, the coarser particles left upon a 40 or 60 mesh sieve frequently revealing the nature of the adulterant or the too large proportion of pepper husk. Afterwards it is well, with a good dissecting microscope and a power of 15 to 30, to sort over the ground pepper, and judge of the frequency of the occurrence of the coarse particles, which after a little experience there will be no difficulty in doing. The presence of sand or a notable excess of P. D. can also be detected and estimated in this simple way. Backgrounds of white and black, with reflected light and afterwards transmitted light, may be used in the manner so conveniently afforded by Zeiss's stand, made for this purpose.

A portion of the powdered pepper or the separated coarse particles should also be treated with chloral-hydrate solution for twenty-four hours, to render it more transparent for examination with higher powers, and in the mean time the coarse particles sieved from the powder may be examined under a one and a one-half inch objective, and then crushed and re-examined, using both plain and polarized light. In this way husky matter may be distinguished and foreign starches detected. Polarized light is then the means of bringing out more plainly the starches, the proportion of which iodine will reveal, making due allowance for the small granules of pepper starch and all optically active tissue, such as the bast fibers and sclerenchyma or stone cells, which are found in olive-stones and cocoa-nut shells.

The structure of the pepper itself, as has been explained, is so characteristic as not to be readily confused with foreign matter. In the chloral hydrate preparation, which should now be examined, much of this disappears as the starch is much swollen by this reagent. The husky matter present is rendered thereby so much clearer on the other hand that its identification and differentiation is made much easier, and it is here that the possibility of fixing the source of the adulterant will often lie.

Experience with a half dozen samples from a cheap grocery in comparison with a laboratory sample of pure pepper will soon teach one the best means of making out what has been briefly described.

It has also been found most valuable to digest about a gram of pepper with nitric acid, sp. gr. 1.1, and chlorate of potash for several hours, or until the color is bleached. It is then possible to distinguish the denser cellular structure more easily than in any other way, particularly the stone cells which make up the larger part of the cocoanut shells and ground olive stones, especially with polarized light, being careful not to confuse the stone cells of the pepper husk with those of olive stones or other adulterants. Charcoal at the same time remains unbleached.

To determine the merits and correctness of the various chemical processes and statements in regard to them previously referred to, a series of pure whole peppers, direct from importers, and of the commercial ground article, have been collected. The results also reveal the extent and nature of the adulteration practiced in this part of the country. The specimens were of the origin described below.

Sources of specimens of pepper.

WHOLE PEPPERS.

No.	Kind.	Remarks.
4514	Whole black....	First quality, probably west coast.
4840	... do	West coast, direct from importer.
4894	...do	Aachen, direct from importer.
4895	... do	West coast, direct from importer.
4896	do	Singapore, direct from importer.
4316	Whole white ...	First quality, source doubtful.
4898	...Do..........	Singapore, direct from importers.
	GROUND PEPPERS.	
4515	Black..........	First quality, grocers' guaranteed pure.
4523	....do	Ground in Washington.
28	....do	Ground in Baltimore.
33	....do	Do.
37	....do	Do.
43	....do	Ground in London, guaranteed
52	....do	Ground in Washington.
53	....do	Do.
4883	....do	Ground in Baltimore, low grade "Best."
4884	....do	Ground in Baltimore, low grade "Pure."
4524	White..........	Ground in Washington.
4544	....do	Ground in London, "Pure."
4555	....do	Ground in Washington.
4882	....do	Ground in Baltimore.

MECHANICAL AND MICROSCOPICAL EXAMINATION.

The weight of the whole peppers and the amount of dirt present, as they are imported, have been given already. In the ground condition they of course displayed the normal structure of the berry, as has been already described. No further reference is necessary, therefore, under this head. In the ground specimens the following peculiarities were noted.

4515. Sifting reveals the presence of pepper stems which should not be present, showing that the pepper was ground without cleaning and an undue proportion of husky matter, unbleached by nitric acid and chlorate.

4523. This specimen is very coarsely ground, a large proportion of husk remaining on the 40-mesh sieve, among which evidence of the presence of maize could be distinguished, and that P. D. in some form must be present.

4528. Sifting separated light chaffy and fibrous matter. The microscope detected yellow corn and its hulls.

4533. This proved of very bad quality, the siftings consisting of bran, roasted shells or charcoal, and corn. The microscope was confirmatory, and the presence of the roasted shells prevented bleaching with Schulze's reagent. This is evidently a P. D. pepper of the worst sort.

4537. Sifting and examination showed the presence of P. D. in some form and corn. It contains no roasted matter or charcoal.

4543. Proved to be quite pure and well ground, all the material passing a 40-mesh and nearly all a 60-mesh sieve. This is the only *pure ground* sample met with.

4552. Sifting shows the presence of a complicated collection of adulterants, husks of various origin, &c. Microscopic examination detected mustard hulls, corn, roasted shells, or charcoal not bleachable, and other foreign material not identified.

4553. Contains mustard hulls and branny matter, but no charcoal. *Bad.*

4883 and 4884. From the same mill in Baltimore were the worst specimens met with. They contained but little pepper and were made up of P. D., yellow corn, cracker dust, cayenne, charcoal, and other foreign matter.

4882. A white pepper from the same source was of the same origin, leaving out the black elements.

4524 and 4544. These white peppers were found to be pure, but the former not carefully decorticated.

4555. Contained foreign starchy matter and probably cayenne. Sifting revealed nothing abnormal.

These examples serve to show the variations which are met with and what the analyist may expect. It is always well, also, to be on one's guard for something new.

As a confirmation of the physical examination and a means of determining the amount of adulteration in the several cases determinations were made of the proximate composition:

Analysis of peppers.

[Whole black.]

Serial number.	Source.	Per cent. of dust.	Weight of 100 grains.	Quality.	Water.	Ash.	Volatile oil.	Piperine and resin.	Alcohol extract.	Starch.	Undetermined.	Crude fiber.	Albuminoids.	Total.	Total N. ×6.25.	Total N.	Reducing sugar equivalent, on dry ash free pepper.
4514	West Coast	Clean	5.960	Cleaned	8.91	4.04	.70	7.29	......	36.52	24.62	10.23	7.69	100	9.8?	1.57	47.16
4840	do	Clean	6.460	Retail	8.15	2.91	1.48	7.20	5.08	33.92	21.02	8.71	11.50	100	13.65	2.18	42.38
4894	Acheen	2.5	4.525	As imported	8.29	4.70	1.69	7.72	6.06	37.50	13.64	10.92	10.38	100	12.60	2.02	47.87
4895	West Coast	4.3	5.085	do	9.36	4.52	1.63	7.90	5.71	36.18	13.59	10.30	10.81	100	13.13	2.10	46.68
4896	Singapore	8.3	4.870	do	9.83	3.70	1.60	7.15	5.74	37.30	17.66	10.02	10.00	100	12.08	1.93	44.13
				[Whole white.]													
4516	West Coast	Clean	5.130	Retail	9.85	1.41	.57	7.24	....	40.61	23.28	7.73	9.31	100	11.48	1.83	50.86
4898	Singapore	1.4	4.960	Imported	10.60	1.34	1.20	7.76	2.57	43.10	19.55	4.20	9.62	100	11.90	1.90	54.38
				[Commercial ground black.]													
4515	Washington grocers			Adulterated	10.00	4.52	.09	6.50	......	31.86	21.53	15.90	9.00	100	10.88	1.74	39.80
4523	do			do	11.83	4.38	1.04	6.59	......	21.56	23.49	10.55	20.56	100	21.88	3.50	28.52
4528	do			do	12.30	6.54	.84	5.94	......	30.60	18.04	15.93	9.51	100	11.20	1.79	40.90
4533	do			do	8.92	4.06	.92	3.99	......	30.83	21.52	20.48	9.28	100	10.23	1.65	39.30
4537	do			do	11.15	7.85	.82	6.59	......	27.85	17.30	19.03	9.31	100	11.20	1.79	38.19
4542	do			Good	10.70	3.85	.42	7.19	......	30.47	20.81	14.90	9.66	100	11.73	1.88	40.57
4562	do			Adulterated	7.60	7.50	2.94	5.92	......	27.01	25.55	11.20	12.25	100	13.95	2.23	35.40
4533	do			do	8.90	9.85	1.14	6.38	......	21.27	27.13	13.53	11.80	100	16.63	2.66	29.08
4883	Baltimore Mills			do	9.48	6.15	2.09	2.66	6.54	28.19	14.83	18.13	11.93	100	12.60	2.02	37.18
4881	do			do	8.45	5.29	1.66	2.80	5.61	31.34	16.36	16.73	11.73	100	12.43	1.99	40.37
				[Commercial ground white.]													
4524	Baltimore Mills			Pure	11.56	1.46	.48	7.11	......	41.06	25.30	5.13	8.26	100	10.33	1.65	52.28
4544	do			do	11.35	1.86	.55	7.45	......	48.29	14.35	4.63	12.52	100	13.80	2.20	59.81
4555	do			do	8.95	1.35	1.25	7.22	......	50.30	16.55	5.98	8.40	100	10.50	1.68	65.73
4882	do			Adulterated	11.12	2.13	.96	2.81	4.10	15.58	4.24	12.13	10.79	100	11.55	1.85	66.09

The analyses of the pure specimens of pepper show that in all the amount of water was between 8 and 10 per cent. This is of course variable with surrounding conditions. The ash in black peppers did not exceed 4.7 per cent., and in white 1.4. It is fair to believe that anything above 5 per cent. for black and 2 per cent. for white is suspicious, otherwise adulteration or dirt are certainly present.

The volatile oil varies in black pepper from 1.69 to .70, and in white 1.26 and .57 were found. This determination is not of great value as a means of detecting adulteration. Piperine and resin, however, furnish a most valuable check on the purity of the samples. In the whole berries ground by us both black and white contained from 7.90 to 7.24 of these substances, showing great constancy in amount, and on the addition of adulterants this is plainly affected. It serves, in my opinion, as well or better than determinations of pure piperine, the latter being difficult and involving loss, as has been shown by careful experiments made by Mr. Knorr under my direction. It has also proved impossible to make determinations of piperine by the combustion or Kjeldahl methods by application of Stützer's copper hydrate process, the per cent. of nitrogen being so small, 4.912 in piperine, as to make the error very large when converting the former to the latter, the necessary factor being 20.36. Rottger's objection to the value of the determination of the ether extract is not sustained in our experience, and it seems that he must have employed inferior ether, which is often the cause of serious error. Only the best Squibb's ether or its equivalent should be used for extractions.

The alcohol extract appears to be of no value.

The determination of starch or its equivalent in reducing sugars has been looked into with care and the conclusions arrived at are that the results are of value when carried out in the manner which has been described under the general head of methods of analysis. A preliminary extraction with alcohol and water is necessary to obtain results which are fairly constant. Determinations made in this way show that black peppers contain from 34 to 38 per cent. of starch, or 42 to 47 per cent. of substances of reducing sugar equivalent calculated on dry ash free substance. White peppers contain in the same way from 40 to 43 per cent. of starch, and give from 50 to 55 per cent. of reducing sugar equivalent on dry ash free substance. These figures are not as high as those given by Lenz, but are the result of careful work on pure samples, extending over a long time and involving much experience. It is believed that they must be nearly correct. In our opinion there is no advantage in calculating the results to a sugar equivalent unless excessive moisture or ash is found to be present.

The crude fiber in the black peppers, as determined by our methods, does not vary far from 10 per cent. One sample contained but 8.74, and of course in the white peppers the amount is much reduced, depending to a certain extent on the perfection of the decortication; 4 to

8 per cent. are probably fair limits. The determination is of comparative value, revealing the presence of foreign woody or fibrous matter.

The albuminoids do not vary widely, 10 per c ent. being the average, with extremes in our experience of 7.69 and 11.50. The addition of nitrogenous seeds of course increases the amount, and of fibrous or woody matter diminishes it. As will be seen, therefore, the determination is a useful one. The variations, then, may be summarized as follows:

	Black.	White.
Water	8.0 to 11.0	8.0 to 11.0
Ash	2.75 to 5.0	1.0 to 2.0
Volatile oil	.50 to 1.75	.50 to 1.75
Piperine and resin	7.0 to 8.0	7.0 to 8.0
Starch	32.0 to 38.0	40.0 to 44.0
Crude fiber	8.0 to 11.0	4.11 to 8.0
Albuminoids	7.0 to 12.0	8.0 to 10.0

With these pure peppers the ground samples must be compared. In the table the determinations which are suspicious are printed in full-faced type. All but one of the black peppers are convicted of adulteration on the chemical evidence.

The first, 4515, has too little piperine and resin, too little starch, and too much fiber. It is apparent that some fibrous or woody diluent has been added, as appears from the microscopic examination to be true.

Without discussing each analysis in detail it may be pointed out that only three samples contained an excess of ash, as a rule being free from mineral adulterants, and the three cases are probably only dirty, so that the addition of minerals is not common in this country.

The piperine and resin were deficient in all the specimens except the one pure one, revealing at once sophistication.

Starch was deficient in all the specimens, in the pure specimen falling below the usual limits, which at the same time was more than usually husky, thus accounting for the difference, and in fact in all but two cases there was present more fiber in the peppers than we have considered normal, another indication of the presence of adulterants or dirt.

The albuminoids in two cases were present in excessive amount, revealing the presence of some foreign seed rich in nitrogen. In the other specimens the adulterants did not throw this determination far away from the normal.

In the white peppers the presence of an excessive amount of starch in 4555 makes it suspicious, and the great deficit in piperine and excess of starch and fiber show that 4882 is adulterated.

The value of the chemical determinations is thus plainly illustrated. Perhaps with no one of the substances which are considered in this report are the indications more certain. It would be possible, too, in an indirect way, by means of proportions such as have been already mentioned, to calculate with an approximation to accuracy the extent of the adulteration. It is fortunate that in a material which is probably more frequently adulterated than any other the presence of foreign matter is so easily detected.

CAYENNE.

Cayenne or red pepper is the powdered pod of several species of *Capsicum*, a genus of the family *Solanaceæ*, to which the potato and tomato belong, the commonest species being *C. annuum* and *C. fastigiatum*, known also under many synonyms.

The first, Flückiger and Hanbury state, furnishes the larger kinds of pod pepper, and, as they believe, much of the cayenne pepper which is imported into England in a state of powder.

C. fastigiatum is the species which is officinal in both the British and United States pharmacopœias. It is grown in tropical Africa and America and appears in our market as Zanzibar pepper. The color of its powder is lighter yellow than that of the preceding. The two species furnish the market with its cayenne pepper, although a few other species are sought in small amount for their peculiar flavor.

Of the microscopic structure Flückiger and Hanbury say:

> The pericarp consists of two layers, the outer being composed of yellow thick-walled cells. The inner layer is twice as broad and exhibits a soft shrunken parenchyme, traversed by thin fibro-vascular bundles. The cells of the outer layer especially are the seat of the fine granular coloring matter. If it is removed by an alcoholic solution of potash, a cell nucleus and drops of fat or oil make their appearance. The structural details of this fruit afford interesting subjects for microscopical investigation.

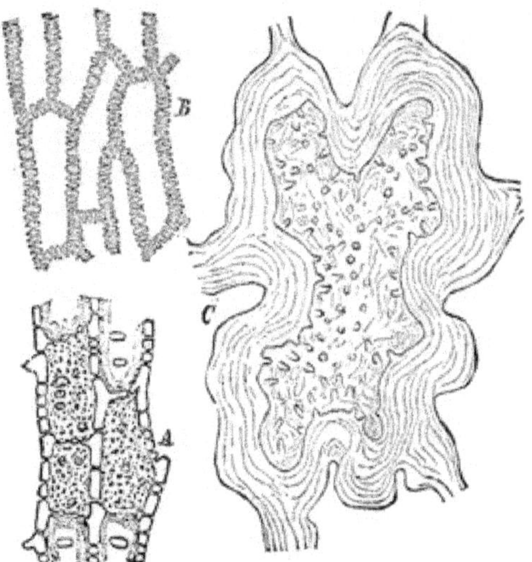

FIG. 12. Cayenne: *A*, outer epidermis. *B*, stone cells of the inner epidermis; *C*, epidermis cells of the edge of seed. (After Schimper.)

The peculiarities described above are so distinctive that the presence of foreign matter is easily detected. The cells of the pericarp or epidermis are of a peculiar flattened and chain-like angular form which are characteristic of cayenne. The other structures are not as prominent, but are not liable to be confounded with those of any adulterants. Diagrammatic representatives of this structure are given in Fig. 12, and the appearance of the pure ground cayenne under polarized light in Fig. 48, Plate XXIV. The portions of the seed in the powder are not readily distinguished without careful examination. They are, however, characteristic and contain starch, the form of which is shown in Fig. 67, Plate XXVII. The adulterants, which are said by Hassall to be more numerous and frequent than with ordinary pepper, are given by authorities as mineral coloring matter added to hide the loss of color which takes place on exposure of cayenne to light, to add to the weight, or to cover the addition of colorless diluents, ground rice, turmeric, husks of mustard, etc.

Mineral adulterants were met with in but one sample of a low grade, obtained in the Baltimore market. The organic ones, on the contrary, were almost always present, among them yellow corn meal being found, but rice or corn flour oftener. The latter was readily detected with the polariscope, as illustrated in Fig. 49, Plate XXIV. The few starch grains in the lower layers of the pericarp and in the seed are very small and cannot be confused with the added rice or corn. Turmeric and mustard are recognized by their peculiar structure.

Of the chemistry of *Capsicum* but little had been written until 1884, when Strohmer undertook an investigation of the proximate composition of the pod. Bracconot had announced the discovery of the active principle, and named it capsicine. Wilting had asserted that it was a crystalline alkaloid. Thresh had discovered a crystalline body capsicine, which he regarded as the substance to which the pungency was due, but Strohmer showed that there was present in the cayenne—

(1) A fixed oil, without sharp smell or taste, that required 201.9 of KOH for saponification and occurred almost entirely in the seed.

(2) A camphor-like substance which tastes and smells sharp, and which constitutes the peculiar principle of the cayenne (capsicine). It is contained in the pods and seeds, although in greater amount in the former than in the latter, where it is dissolved in a fixed oil.

(3) A resinous body, the red coloring matter, (capsicum red) which is only contained in the pod.

Quantitative determinations were made of the fruit of *Capsicum annuum*, grown in Hungary.

The percentage of water given is probably too high, owing to the volatilization of the camphor-like substance.

The ether extract of the seed was nearly pure fat, that of the pod capsicum red.

As to whether a pepper is adulterated or not, Strohmer considers that these determinations will furnish the evidence. He found in commercial Cayennes:

	(I) Rosen-paprika, prima.	(II) Rosen-paprika, sekunda.	(III) König's, paprika.
Water	17.35	14.39	12.69
Albuminoids	14.56	14.31	13.19
Ether extract	14.43	15.06	13.35
Ash	5.10	5.66	7.14

The latter specimen was adulterated with stems, &c., and the results show the agreement between the degeneration in quality and the analytical determinations.

In our investigations several specimens have been examined with the following results:

4517. English brand.
4545. New York brand.
4554. Bulk, corner grocery.
4554.[1] Public lunch-room.
4880. Baltimore spice mills.
4881. Baltimore spice mills.
4897. Zanzibar; pure, whole, from importers.

Microscopic examination.

4517. Pure, Crosse and Blackwells. Bottled.
4545. Adulterated rice flour.
4554. Adulterated rice flour.
4554.[1] Adulterated rice flour.
4880. Adulterated } yellow corn, turmeric, and red ocher.
4881. Adulterated } yellow corn, turmeric, and red ocher.

The analytical results were:

Serial No.	Water.	Ash.	Fixed oil.	Volatile camphor, &c.	Fiber.	Albuminoids.	Undetermined.	Total.	Nitrogen.	Quality.
4897	2.35	9.06	0.12	26.99	16.88	13.13	41.47	100.00	2.10	Pure.
4517	5.74	5.24	1.58	17.00	18.10	11.20	40.24	100.00	1.79	Do.
4515	3.70	6.16	3.40	14.50	15.40	10.15	46.75	100.00	1.62	Adulterated.
4554	5.20	6.65	1.65	14.11	10.52	9.98	51.88	100.00	1.60	Do.
4880	1.41	4.68	4.00	9.41	14.70	7.70	58.10	100.00	1.23	Do.
4881	1.93	8.69	3.48	6.66	13.33	7.00	58.91	100.00	1.12	Do.

From the data it is not difficult to detect the presence of adulterants. The whole Zanzibar pepper ground in the laboratory has 26.99 per cent. of non-volatile ether extract, much more than was found by Strohmer, and the other pure specimen 17.90 per cent. None of the others reach these figures. In albuminoids the addition of starchy and mineral diluents also makes a marked difference, their presence being revealed in a striking way.

The unexplained presence of so much volaltile matter on the two worst specimens and of so much ash in the Zanzibar of good grade as compared with these same specimens containing mineral adulterants, is remarkable and shows that too hasty conclusions must not be drawn from the chemical data. It should be noticed also that the water in our specimens falls far below that given by Strohmer, a peculiarity which has been noted in other cases. In the detection of adulteration of Cayenne by chemical methods, determinations of water and ash, ether extract and albuminoids are, it seems, of value and as a rule will serve to reveal the means of adulteration. When combined with a microscopic examination the estimation of the amount of the diluents present would not be difficult.

GINGER.

The rhizome, or commonly root, of *Zingiber officinale* is known as ginger. It is a "reed-like plant, with annual leafy stems 3 to 4 feet high, and flowers in cone-shaped spikes borne on other stems thrown up from the rhizome. It is a native of Asia, in the warmer countries of which it is universally cultivated, but is not known in the wild state. It has been introduced into most tropical countries, including the West Indies."

Ginger occurs in two forms—dried with the epidermis as coated ginger and as scraped ginger when the epidermis is removed. The uncoated ginger is prepared by scraping and washing the rhizome and then drying it in the sun. Thus prepared, Flückiger and Hanbury say:

> It has a pale buff hue and breaks easily, exhibiting a short and farinaceous fracture with numerous bristle-like fibers. When cut with a knife the younger and terminal portion of the rhizome appears pale yellow, soft, and amylaceous, while the older part is flinty, hard, and resinous.
>
> Coated ginger or that which has been dried without the removal of the epidermis is covered with a wrinkled, striated brown integument, which imparts to it a somewhat coarse and crude appearance, which is usually remarkably less developed on the flat parts of the rhizome. Internally it is usually of a less bright and delicate hue than ginger from which the cortical part has been removed. Much of it, indeed, is dark, horny, and resinous.

In our markets we find Jamaica ginger, which is the finest variety, being very carefully prepared and scraped, and several qualities of brown ginger which is unscraped and not carefully prepared, and is imported from India and the East. The latter is sometimes bleached and coated with gypsum or carbonate of lime to improve its appearance. This method of treatment appears to be very common.

Of the microscopic appearance of the rhizome Flückiger and Hanbury write as follows:

A transverse section of coated ginger exhibits a brown, horny external layer, about one millimetre broad, separated by a fine line from the whitish mealy interior portion, through the tissue of which numerous vascular bundles and resin cells are irregularly scattered. The external tissue consists of a loose outer layer, and an inner composed of tabular cells; these are followed by peculiar short prosenchymatous cells the walls of which are sinuous on transverse section and partially thickened, imparting a horny appearance. This delicate felted tissue forms the striated surface of scraped ginger and is the principal seat of the resin and volatile oil, which here fill large spaces. The large-celled parenchyme which succeeds is loaded with starch and likewise contains numerous masses of resin and drops of oil. The starch granules are irregularly spherical, attaining at the utmost 40^{mm}. Certain varieties of ginger, owing to the starch having been rendered gelatinous by scalding, are throughout horny and translucent. The circle of vascular bundles which separates the outer layers and the central portion is narrow and has the structure of the corresponding circle or nucleus sheath on turmeric.

In the best ground ginger of the trade little is seen of this structure. The appearance is one of predominating starch grains which are so abundant in the parenchyma, and which are figured in Plate XXI, Fig. 41, and Plate XXVII, Fig. 58. They are so characteristic in shape and in their appearance with polarized light, that they are readily distinguished from adulterations.

Among them are seen scattered the fibro-vascular bundles, the turmeric-like resin bodies, and less prominently the oil globules, which are few in number.

When the source of the powder is the ordinary unscraped ginger, the outer horny layer is prominent, but not distinct in its character, and at times when the rhizome has been scalded the starch grains are swollen and the whole structure is more difficult to make out. It is not, however, as a rule, difficult to detect foreign matter in the powder of this spice.

ADULTERANTS.

The principal adulterants are said to be mineral matter, sago, tapioca, flour of rice, wheat, and potato, cayenne, mustard hulls, turmeric, and exhausted ginger. The foreign starches, cayenne, and mustard hulls, are easily detected, but the turmeric cells, from their resemblance to the resin globules of the ginger, are more confusing. The too frequent occurrence of such cells is suspicious. For the detection of exhausted ginger recourse must be had to proximate analysis. The recommendation also of Hassall, to wash away some of the starch, or the use of a sieve, will be found of advantage, the remaining coarse particles being then seen in greater numbers and with more ease. We have found in the gingers of the trade rice flour, turmeric, and hulls of foreign seeds. But two of the specimens were derived from coated root.

CHEMICAL COMPOSITION.

Owing to the practice of diluting the ground spice with the residues from extraction for turmeric, &c., the normal proximate composition is of importance.

W. C. Young* has examined seven well-authenticated specimens with results which have been reprinted here.

Sources.	Moisture at 100° C.	Ash.	Ash, insoluble in H_2O.	Ash, soluble in H_2O.	Aqueous extract, 2 per cent. decoction.	Mucilage.	Alcohol extract, 5 per cent. decoction.	Resin.	Cellulose
African 1	15.8	3.4	1.34	2.06	24.8	18.0	8.5	2.2	5.1
African 2	14.5	4.3	1.58	2.72	52.2	......	15.7	......	......
Jamaica	15.0	5.4	1.22	4.18	55.7	32.3	6.5	.25	3.1
Cochin	15.2	5.8	3.28	2.52	35.1	21.8	12.5	4.5	8.0
Japan	15.2	8.0	5.82	2.18	34.3	19.4	8.3	2.8	4.6
Malabar	10.2	3.4	1.6	1.8	30.1	22.4	4.1	1.7	1.7
Bengal	20.50	4.75	2.36	2.39	51.4	41.1	4.3	.84	4.9

These specimens were all scraped with the exception of the last two. The analyses do not seem to have been carried out on accepted principles, and are not of great value except for ash and perhaps fiber, but in complete want of any data they have been copied. The fact that the decorticated specimens contain no more fiber than the others is peculiar. The methods of determining "resin" and "mucilage" and the meaning of the terms also are not given. Little is therefore learned from them.

Tresh† has investigated the ether extract of the rhizome, but his results furnish us with no data of analytical use. Lately E. W. T. Jones‡ has, under the title "The Amount of Starch in Ground Ginger," obtained some data which are of value, but unfortunately are confined to only one specimen of ginger. He determined water and ash as usual, extracted with ether, after moistening with alcohol (Sp. gr 0.90), at 35°–38°, and with water at the same temperature. The residue, after gelatinizing the starch, was submitted to diastatic action. In the filtrate from the unacted-upon substance, which was weighed as fiber, the dextrine and maltose were determined by the polariscope. Fiber was also determined by the usual method of treatment with acid and alkali. The results were:

*Analyst, **9**, 214–215, 1884.

† Pharm. J., Trans., **37**, 610, 721, 1882.

‡ Analyst, **11**, 75–77, 1886.

	Per cent.
Moisture, loss at 100° C	10.10
Ether extract	3.58
Alcohol extract	3.38
Water extract	3.66
Starch, calc., from dextrine and maltose	52.92
Fiber, residue from diastatic action	19.12
Crude fiber by acid and alkali	2.66
Ash	4.80
Matter not accounted for in the starch products	1.50
	99.06

Practically we have learned from all that has been hitherto done in the proximate examination of ginger that the ash may vary from 3.4 to 8.0 per cent. in genuine samples, and fiber from 1.7 to 9.0 per cent. Young and Jones differ altogether too much on other points to be of any value. We are therefore in need of further information to enable us to detect the addition of spent ginger as an adulterant, the differences in determinations of fiber being so wide as to render this determination of no value, since it is possible to even reduce the amount of fiber by such an addition and judicious selection.

With a view to extending our knowledge of the subject we have examined a number of pure gingers, obtained from the importers and several samples of ginger found in the local markets, some of which, as was learned from the microscopic examination, were adulterated with farinaceous matter and foreign hulls. The results were:

Analyses of gingers.

Sources of samples:

4506. Scraped Jamaica, limed, whole.
4889. Whole Calcutta ginger root, unscraped and unbleached.
4890. Whole Cochin ginger root, unscraped and unbleached.
4891. Whole Jamaica ginger root, unscraped and unbleached.
4892. Whole Jamaica ginger root, London market, bleached.
4893. Whole Jamaica ginger root, American market, bleached.
4507. White ground Jamaica, "pure."
4521. Brown, ground in Washington.
4526. Brown, ground in Baltimore.
4541. Genuine Borneo, English brand.
4549. Brown.
4242. Mohawk, N. Y.
4875. Ground ginger, Baltimore Spice Mills, "pure."
4876. Ground ginger, Baltimore Spice Mills, "best."

Microscopical examination:

4506 and 4889–4893. Pure standards.
4507. Not as much fiber matter as in the preceding, but no adulterants detected.
4521. Good brown ginger.
4526. Starch, turmeric, and foreign husks.
4541. Good and white.
4549. Starch, and perhaps turmeric; brown.
4242. Starch and some questionable substance.
4875 and 4876. Cereals and cayenne; perhaps exhausted ginger.

Analyses of gingers.

[Whole ginger root.]

Serial No.	Source.	Water.	Ash.	Volatile oil.	Fixed oil and resin.	Starch.	Crude fiber.	Albuminoids.	Undetermined.	Total.	Nitrogen.
4889	Calcutta	9.60	7.02	2.27	4.58	49.34	7.45	6.30	13.44	100	1.01
4890	Cochin	9.41	3.39	1.84	4.07	53.33	2.05	7.00	18.91	100	1.12
4891	Unbleached Jamaica	10.49	3.44	2.03	2.29	50.58	4.74	10.85	13.58	100	1.74
4892	Bleached Jamaica, London	11.00	4.54	1.89	3.04	49.34	1.70	9.28	19.21	100	1.48
4893	Bleached Jamaica, American	10.11	5.58	2.54	2.69	50.67	7.65	9.10	11.66	100	1.46
4506	Bleached Jamaica	9.10	4.36	.96	3.09	46.16	3.15	5.25	27.93	100	.84

[Commercial ground.]

Serial No.	Source.	Quality.	Water.	Ash.	Volatile oil.	Fixed oil and resin.	Starch.	Crude fiber.	Albuminoids.	Undetermined.	Total.	Nitrogen.
4507	Bleached	Pure	8.06	3.47	1.78	**3.11**	48.92	2.65	6.13	25.88	100	.98
4521	Unbleached	....	11.20	6.02	1.61	**4.12**	50.00	4.08	6.28	16.69	100	1.04
4526	do	Adulterated	10.25	5.82	1.52	**4.66**	46.49	3.48	8.75	18.92	100	1.40
4541	do	....	8.90	3.45	.95	**3.63**	49.12	3.45	6.30	24.18	100	1.01
4549	do	Adulterated	9.45	4.75	1.45	**4.30**	50.58	4.29	8.93	16.34	100	1.43
4575	Brown	do	11.82	7.34	2.61	**3.21**	46.43	4.98	7.35	18.29	100	1.18
4576	do	do	11.33	7.94	2.11	**3.51**	**49.12**	3.79	7.35	15.44	100	1.18

From these results it appears that the ash is quite variable, a pure sample having as much as 7.02 per cent. and as little as 3.44 per cent., the whiter varieties having the least and the brown the most. From the ether extract little can be learned. There is no distinction even between the pure and adulterated, the adulterations having a very similar amount of extract. Of the pure samples the white has the least, as well as the least ash. Of fiber the least, as would naturally be expected, is found in the whitest and best scraped and prepared varieties. Of albuminoids it may be said that there is no greater variation in the pure samples than in those which proved to be adulterated. When foreign hulls are present the amount may be much larger. The determinations of starch do not show that the samples have been diluted with cereals or any farinaceous matter, neither could any be detected under the microscope.

The chemical examination proves consequently most unsatisfactory, and it is only possible to give the following hints for pure ginger:

In our markets ginger is drier than abroad, as is usually the fact with all such substances in our climate. The percentage of ash among Young's samples reached 8.0, but did not go below our lowest determination, and our variations in fiber include his figures and those of Tresh.

In other respects our determinations agree with those of the two investigators mentioned, and from their increased number serve as a fair basis for comparison.

A careful qualitative examination of the character of the extracts at times may reveal the presence of an adulterant, but the chief dependence must, it seems, in the examination of this spice, be placed upon the microscope. This, however, will not reveal the presence of exhausted ginger, and a careful study of the effect of exhaustion on the proximate composition of the ground root is therefore desirable. It would naturally increase the relative of percentages of fiber and albuminoids and starch and diminish that of extractive matter.

CINNAMON AND CASSIA

Cinnamon and cassia are the barks of several species of the genus *Cinnamomum*, the true cinnamon (*C. zeylanicum*) being a native of Ceylon, where it is also largely cultivated, while the cassias are derived from several species growing in Bengal and in the countries east of India, especially China and in the Indian Archipelago. In our markets the Chinese and Malabar cassias occupy the most prominent place, Batavia and various other localities supplying a poorer quality. Ceylon cinnamon is only found in small amount and usually is in use as a drug. In our experience it is not to be procured in a ground condition. In their original form there is no difficulty in identifying the various barks by their peculiar characteristics. Ceylon cinnamon, during its preparation, is deprived of its outer corky coat and of the inner cortical layers. It is therefore thin, not more than one-eighth to one-sixteenth inch thick, and is distinguished by having the quills, which curl inward on each side, arranged one within the other, forming a flattened cylinder, originally a yard long. Its color is a dull brown, and the removal of the outer coats is discovered by the appearance on the exterior of the peculiar wavy structure of the inner layers of the bark.

Cassia, on the other hand, commonly shows the outer corky coat of the bark, and is, in consequence, much thicker, rougher, and of not so red color. In some cases, however, the bark is scraped, but the character of the surfaces are still distinctly marked, and it is thicker and deeper in color than cinnamon.

Microscopically, true cinnamon consists of thin layers, which in the ground drug are represented most prominently by the long cells of woody fiber or liber fibers which are scattered through the bark, and which are distinctly seen under polarized light, the stellate cells of the outer layers and the thinner cells of the interior carrying the few starch grains. In cassia, which of course bears a close general resemblance to cinnamon, the woody fiber is comparatively small in amount, as is the number of the stellate cells. The presence of starch is, on the other hand, more marked. A view, therefore, of a true ground cinnamon and cassia with polarized light reveals at once differences which are characteristic enough to distinguish the specimens, and which are illustrated in figures 46 and 47, plate XXIV. In the ground specimens which we have had in hand, however, no specimens of true cinnamon have been found. Reference was made, therefore, to ground samples prepared from authentic specimens of Ceylon and Chinese barks, and before any microscopic work is attempted it is necessary to make a comparative examination of this description to acquire a knowledge of the appearances to be expected and which cannot be described in detail. Reference may also be usefully made to Flückiger and Hanbury, Pharmacographia, for many details in regard to the growth, cultivation, preparation, &c.

Of the addition of cedar sawdust, roasted hulls, oil meals, and mineral and coloring matter we have had but little opportunity to judge. Adulteration in these markets is mainly confined to replacing cinnamon by cassia, and the adulterants mentioned are found only in the lowest grades, while their entire difference in structure make their detection microscopically a matter of no difficulty.

Schimper in his *Anleitung zur mikroskopischen Untersuchung der Nahrungs- und Genussmittel*, describes in detail the appearance of these foreign substances which in Germany seem to be often used and which Wood in Massachusetts has detected in the forms of ground crackers and nut shells, and in Canada are represented by ground peas and wheat, flour, and, as we have found in Baltimore, by minerals and coloring matter. As will be shown, the determination of fiber and ash are valuable means of discovering the presence of such additions.

CHEMICAL COMPOSITION AND REACTION.

Of the proximate composition of any of the barks but little is known. Numerous determinations and analyses of the ash have been made with a view to detecting peculiarities or the addition of mineral matter.

Hilger* has recently found in five samples of Ceylon cinnamon the following amounts of ash :

	Soluble—per ct.
(1)—4.5	53.0
(2)—4.8	72.3
(3)—3.9	88.1
(4)—4.3	61.7
(5)—3.4	....

Hehner† in 1879 made an extended investigation into the substitution of cassia for cinnamon, and examined the iodine test, finding it useless, as has been the case when employed in our laboratory. He then investigated the mineral constituents, thinking that the more woody cassia

*Arch. d. Pharm., **223**, 826.

†Analyst, **I**. 223-228.

bark would contain more lime and magnesia than the more delicate cinnamon. Some of his figures are as follows:

Kind.	Price per pound, retail.	Moisture.	Ash in bark.	Lime in ash.	Mn^3O^4.	Soluble ash.	Insoluble ash.
	s. d.						
Whole cinnamon	1 10	12.67	4.78	40.09	.86	25.04	74.96
	3 0	12.05	4.59	36.98	.97	28.98	71.02
	3 6	11.38	4.66	40.39	.13	25.22	74.78
	3 6	11.64	3.44	34.32	.62	26.36	73.64
	8 6	12.94	4.28	36.99	.59	27.67	72.33
Cinnamon chips	*9	11.25	4.44	42.11	.34	18.34	81.66
Cassia lignea:							
Whole		14.22	1.84	25.29	5.11	40.58	59.42
		11.88	2.54	34.49	4.94	26.78	72.22
Ground		11.05	2.55	28.63	3.55	30.91	69.09
Cassia vera		10.37	4.08	52.72	1.13	8.36	91.64
		11.36	4.85	43.40	1.53	15.89	84.11

*Containing wood.

From these analyses Hehner concludes that the ash in cinnamon varies between comparatively narrow limits. *Cassia vera*, or Malabar cassia, contains as much as cinnamon, *Cassia lignea* less; that one quarter of the ash is soluble in water in cinnamon, less in *C. vera*, and still less in *C. lignea;* that cinnamon ash contains less than 1 per cent. of oxide of manganese, *C. vera* more than 1 per cent., and *C. lignea* far more, even up to 5 per cent. This is the most noteworthy feature and is shown in the color of the ash, cinnamon ash being white, while those of cassias are gray or brown. *Cassia vera*, the Malabar cassia, is not so readily distinguished from cinnamon as *C. lignea*, but its occurrence is less frequent. The percentages of lime and magnesia were not distinctive, as had been expected. For cinnamon, 40.09, 36.98, and 40.39 were the amounts of lime in three specimens. In one of *Cassia lignea* 25.29 per cent. was found. In one of *C. vera*, 52.72. The less fibrous *C. lignea* contained the least lime. Of magnesia there was 2.65, 3.30, and 3.86 in the cinnamon and 5.48 and 1.10 in the *Cassia lignea* and *vera* respectively. Little seems to have been learned, therefore, which would form a sound basis for distinguishing these barks. The presence of manganese is more or less accidental and cannot be considered as an essential element of the ash or one from which such definite conclusions could be drawn as to serve as the basis of legal testimony. Our results, in fact, failed to show any large amount in any of the specimens.

Of the proximate organic constituents, the presence of volatile oil, tannin, mucilage, coloring matter, resin, an acid, starch, and lignin is noted by Hassall, without any details in regard to their proportions. The essential oil, according to Pharmacographia, however, amounts to only one-half to 1 per cent. of the bark of cinnamon and must be less in the inferior cassias. Beyond this no data are found. We have examined a number of specimens of the ground bark bearing different designations and three or four samples of bark obtained unground and several authenticated specimens direct from the importers. The sources and descriptions of the material examined were:

DENOMINATED CINNAMON.

4502. Bark from grocers, D. C. Poor quality.
4503. Ground, from same grocers. Both guaranteed, pure.
4519. Ground in Washington, 30 cents per ½ pound.
4529. Ground in Baltimore, 20 cents per ½ pound.
4531. Ground in Baltimore, 30 cents per ½ pound.
4539. Genuine Java cinnamon (cassia), English, 10 cents per ¼ pound.
4547. Cinnamon, Java, ground in Washington.
4556. Ceylon cinnamon bark. Druggists.
4558. Ceylon cinnamon bark. Druggists, 15 cents per ounce.
4868. Cinnamon, pure, Baltimore, Md.
4869. Cinnamon, best, Baltimore, Md.

DENOMINATED CASSIA.

4557. Cassia bark. Druggists.
4559. Cassia bark, 10 cents per ounce. Druggists.
4640. Cassia bark, 10 cents per ounce. Druggists.
4906. Saigon cassia chips, collected in Baltimore markets by Z. D. Gilman.
4907. Cassia ligna bark, collected in Baltimore markets by Z. D. Gilman.
4908. Batavia bark, collected in Baltimore markets by Z. D. Gilman.
4909. Saigon cassia bark, collected in Baltimore markets by Z. D. Gilman.

A mechanical and microscopic examination showed that the ground specimens were hardly what they were represented to be.

4503, guaranteed pure cinnamon, proved to be a good quality of ground cassia.

4519 and 4529 consisted of substitution of cassia for cinnamon.

4531 was a low grade cassia mixed with considerable foreign material.

4539 was an excellent specimen of good cassia.

4547 was a poor quality cassia, adulterated with foreign material, but so finely ground as to make its identification impossible.

4868 and 4869, although labeled cinnamon, were mixtures of the lowest grade, consisting of cassia, turmeric ochre in small amount, mustard hulls or those of a similar seed, cracker dust, and burnt shells.

The remaining specimens were purchased unground, and, with the exception of the one English brand labeled Java cinnamon (cassia), no ground cassia could be purchased under such a designation.

The data obtained in a chemical way were as follows:

Analyses of cinnamon and cassia.

Serial No.	Description.	Sold as—	Consisting of—	Price per pound.	Water.	Ash.	Volatile oil.	Fixed oil, &c.	Crude fiber.	Albuminoids.	Undetermined.	Total.	Nitrogen.
				Cents.									
4502	Ceylon bark				10.60	3.70	3.14	3.30	16.18	3.80	59.88	100	.61
4536	do			*15	5.40	4.55	1.05	1.66	33.08	2.98	51.28	100	.48
4558	do			*15	7.93	3.40	.82	1.58	25.63	3.80	56.84	100	.62
4557	Cassia bark				9.42	2.35	.58	1.40	17.73	2.80	65.72	100	.45
4559	do			*15	9.01	1.75	.84	1.75	20.63	2.45	63.57	100	.39
4640	Buds			40	4.79	5.58	3.59	5.21	8.60	7.00	65.23	100	1.12
4906†	Cassia bark			10	9.49	8.23	1.01	2.13	26.29	4.20	48.65	100	.67
4907‡	do			09	11.04	2.48	1.21	1.86	15.45	2.63	65.33	100	.42
4908§	do			10	17.45	5.25	.55	.74	14.33	4.03	63.65	100	.64
4909‖	do			42	9.32	5.86	3.51	2.38	16.95	4.55	57.43	100	.73
4503	Commercial ground bark	Cinnamon	Cassia		5.60	4.80	3.70	3.92	29.88	2.00	56.10	100	.33
4519	do	do	do	60	9.37	3.36	.96	2.46	18.85	2.28	62.72	100	.36
4529	do	do	do	40	9.51	3.42	1.19	2.69	15.73	2.63	64.83	100	.42
4531	do	do	do	40	7.76	2.92	1.37	1.92	16.43	2.98	66.62	100	.48
4539	do	Cassia	Cassia	1.20	5.19	5.65	4.41	3.70	19.10	3.15	58.80	100	.50
4547	do	do	C. mixtures	40	6.45	2.50	1.00	1.96	18.43	2.10	63.56	100	.34
4868	do	do	do	16	8.73	4.02	1.90	2.86	16.88	4.55	61.06	100	.73
4869	do	do	do	14	11.21	3.74	1.15	2.13	19.18	4.20	58.39	100	.67

* Per ounce. † Saigon chips. ‡ Lignea bark. § Batavia bark. ‖ Saigon bark.

The preceding figures show that there is nothing particularly distinctive between the cinnamons and cassias, and that the determination of volatile oil points more to the character and value of the bark than any other, though, at the same time, there is nothing distinctive therein, as the variation in amount is so large in the cinnamons as to at times furnish samples containing far less volatile oil than even a fair cassia. The percentage of ash is extremely variable, depending on the age and quality of the bark. Saigon chips were found to have 8.23 per cent., while a specimen of unidentified cassia bark had only 1.75 per cent. Cinnamon bark will probably average less than cassia. Fiber, like ash, is extremely variable, and for the same reasons; 26.29 per cent. were found in Saigon chips and 33.08 per cent. in a cinnamon and from 14 to 20 in ordinary cassias. This determination, therefore, reveals nothing, and is of no assistance in detecting adulterants.

Albuminoids are variable, but within narrow limits, the extremes being 4.55 per cent. in Saigon bark and 2.45 in an unidentified cassia. The Batavia and Saigon barks appear to contain the most, over four per cent., and this percentage would seem to be an indication of *inferior quality.*

The amount of tannin in these barks is extremely small, not reaching in our specimens an equivalent of quercitannic acid by the Löwenthal process of two per cent. The addition, therefore, of material containing tannin can be readily detected, but in no case under our observation did such an addition occur.

Aside from the determination of volatile oil, chemical analysis seems to be of little value. The principal dependence must, with our present knowledge, be placed on the mechanical and microscopic examination, since the worst mixtures, 4868 and 4869, scarcely revealed in their composition the fact of their inferiority.

CLOVES.

Cloves are the flower-buds of an evergreen tree, *Eugenia caryophyllata*, growing wild in the Malaccas and introduced into Amboyna, the neighboring Zanzibar islands, Cayenne, and a few other places in the tropics. They are picked by hand when their development has reached a red color, and are dried in the sun, becoming dark brown. They are classed as East Indian, African, and American, and are valued in that order.

Flückiger and Hanbury's description of them is as follows:

Cloves are about six-tenths of an inch in length, and consist of a long cylindrical calyx dividing above into four pointed spreading sepals which surround four petals, closely imbricated as a globular bud about two-tenths of an inch in diameter.

The petals, which are of a lighter color than the rest of the drug and somewhat translucent from numerous oil cells, spring from the base of a four-sided epigynous disc, the angles of which are directed toward the lobes the calyx. The stamens, which are very numerous, are inserted at the base of the petals and are arched over the style. The latter, which is short and subulate, rises from a depression in the center of the disc. Immediately below it, and united with the upper portion of the calyx, is the ovary, which is two-celled and contains many ovules. The lower end of the calyx (hypantium) has a compressed form; it is solid, but has its internal tissue far more porous than the walls. The whole calyx is of a deep rich brown, has a dull wrinkled surface, a dense fleshy texture, and abounds in essential oil, which exudes on simple pressure with the nail.

The varieties of cloves occurring in commerce do not exhibit any structural differences. Inferior kinds are distinguished by being less plump, less bright in tint, and less rich in essential oil. In London price-currents cloves are enumerated in the order of value thus: Penang, Bencoolen (Sumatra), Amboyna, Zanzibar.

A transverse section of the lower part of a clove shows a dark rhomboid zone, the tissue on either side of which is of a lighter hue. The outer layer beneath the epidermis exhibits a large number of oil cells, frequently as much as 300 micromillimeters in diameter. About 200 oil cells may be counted in one transverse section, so that the large amount of essential oil in the drug is well shown by its microscopic characters. The above-mentioned zone is chiefly made up of about 30 fibro-vascular bundles, another stronger bundle traversing the center of the clove. The fibro-vascular bundles, as well as the tissue bordering the oil cells, assume a greenish-black hue by alcoholic perchloride of iron. Oil cells are also largely distributed in the leaves, petals, and even stamens of *Eugenia*. No starch is found in it, however.

Preparations from whole cloves enable one to familiarize himself with the structure, which in the ground cloves is recognized with greater difficulty. In both cases the use of chloral hydrate solution is desirable, as the sections and fragments are otherwise not transparent. Preliminary examination of the powder in water for starch should, however, be made, as the starch granules swell in the chloral hydrate solution.

Among the fragments will be seen a large amount of débris of no apparent structure, but the larger pieces are chiefly the cells of the epidermis interspersed with the large oil cavities or cells, which are not as readily detected as in carefully prepared sections, being concealed by a layer of the epidermal cells. Next in prominence are the fibro-vascular bundles with their spiral vessels and with shreds of deep brown cellular matter attached. Pollen grains and, at times, whole anthers are present, and concretions of oxalate of lime. All these characteristic appearances are made out much more easily under polarized light, the long cells of the fibro-vascular bundles being optically active, as are also the pollen grains, oxalate of lime to a less degree, and the contents of the oil cells which are thus easily distinguished.

After a study of standard powder of cloves, the presence of adulterants is not difficult to recognize. Pimento is often added, and may be identified by the starch which it contains and the characters described under that spice.

Clove stems are said to be the commonest adulterant, and the presence in them of thick-walled stone cells and long yellow fibrous tissue serves as a means of recognition, since similar structures are not found in the clove, at least in the same abundance. The fruit of the clove is also added, and since it contains starch and a large embryo they are detected readily. We have not met either of these adulterants.

In the cheaper forms of ground cloves, where from the price it is evident that adulteration has been practiced, the common substitutes, which are added as diluents to all the spices, must be sought for and require no further experience beyond what has been obtained in the examination of pepper.

In most of the samples which were examined during the preparation of this report the microscope revealed nothing foreign, and for a decision as to their quality it was necessary to have recourse to chemical analysis. Two specimens from Baltimore of the same low grade as several of the spices previously mentioned were found, however, to be mixtures of all sorts of cheap material, containing mineral coloring matter, roasted shells or charcoal, corn, and hulls of seeds.

The sources of the cloves examined were as follows, being largely the ordinary article for sale at grocers:

SOURCES OF CLOVES.

4504. Whole cloves, guaranteed, Washington.
4903. Amboyna cloves, whole, direct from importers.
4904. Singapore cloves, whole, direct from importers.
4905. Clove stems, whole, direct from importers.
4641. Whole cloves, druggists', 10 cents per ounce.
4642. Whole cloves, druggists', 10 cents per ounce.
4643. Whole cloves, druggists', 10 cents per ounce.
4505. Ground cloves, guaranteed, Washington.
4520. Ground gloves, ground in Washington.
4540. Ground cloves, genuine Amboyna, 30 cents per ½ pound; English brand.
4548. Ground cloves, Washington grocers, second class, 26 cents per ½ pound.
4629. Ground cloves, Washington grocers, second class, 20 cents per ½ pound.
4630. Ground cloves, Washington grocers, 30 cents per pound.
4631. Ground cloves, "strictly pure," 40 cents per pound.
4632. Ground cloves, Washington grocers, second class, 30 cents per pound.
4633. Ground cloves, Washington grocers, second class, 30 cents per pound.
4873. Ground cloves, Baltimore Spice Mills; "pure."
4874. Ground cloves, Baltimore Spice Mills; "best."

The results of the analyses are as follows:

Analyses of cloves.

[Whole cloves.]

Serial No.	Source.	Weight of 100 cloves in grams.	Quality.	Water.	Ash.	Volatile oil.	Fixed oil and resin.	Crude fiber.	Albuminoids.	Nitrogen.	Oxygen equivalent.	As quercitannic acid.	Price per ¼ pound.
4504	Grocers			6.95	5.99	16.35	7.12	9.75	4.73	.76	4.06	15.86	
4641	Druggists			3.98	9.31	16.61	9.72	6.94	6.48	1.04	4.73	18.46	$0 40
4642	......do			5.96	7.66	10.23	9.94	8.70	6.48	1.04	5.13	20.02	40
4643	......do			2.90	13.05	15.87	10.07	8.55	7.00	1.12	3.00	11.70	40
4751	Extra quality			8.67	7.72	17.94	9.54	7.83	5.60	.90	5.43	21.19	
4903	Amboyna	10.505		8.78	5.25	18.89	10.24	6.18	5.42	.87	4.80	18.72	
4904	Singapore	8.710		10.67	5.50	13.52	9.95	9.08	5.42	.87	5.67	22.13	
4905	Stems			10.18	6.96	4.40	4.03	13.58	5.78	.92	5.96	23.24	

[Commercial ground cloves.]

Serial No.	Source.	Weight of 100 cloves in grams.	Quality.	Water.	Ash.	Volatile oil.	Fixed oil and resin.	Crude fiber.	Albuminoids.	Nitrogen.	Oxygen equivalent.	As quercitannic acid.	Price per ¼ pound.
4505			Fair	5.93	5.79	13.93	6.74	9.38	5.34	.86	5.60	21.84	
4520			Poor quality	8.86	5.98	9.88	6.88	11.75	4.20	.78	4.80	18.72	15
4543			......do	8.30	5.85	12.40	6.58	11.10	4.38	.70	6.20	24.18	15
4548			......do	8.79	6.05	10.21	7.44	10.93	4.38	.70	5.40	21.84	13
4629			......do	8.78	8.48	8.45	5.36	10.75	5.95	.95	6.07	23.66	10
4630			......do	9.58	10.73	6.52	4.94	12.30	5.78	.92	4.90	19.11	*30
4631			......do	7.48	7.75	12.67	6.74	10.00	6.48	1.04	5.20	20.28	*40
4632			......do	8.71	7.75	3.94	4.02	13.80	5.95	.95	2.89	[illegible]	15
4633			......do	7.99	8.75	7.31	5.20	12.25	5.60	.90	5.33	21.58	10
4873			Adulterated	11.00	9.59	4.06	4.46	17.58	5.42	.87	3.00	11.70	*24
4874			......do	8.62	8.35	3.59	4.47	17.78	5.08	.81	2.96	11.54	*21

* Per pound.

In comparison with these results it is of interest to refer to what has been already published.

Fluckiger states that from 16 to 20 per cent. of volatile oil is present, and gives details in regard to its composition and reactions; but beyond this nothing.

Dietsch gives the following figures as the percentages of oil to be expected in cloves from different sources:

	Per cent.
Amboyna	16 to 21
Zanzibar	12 to 17
Cayenne	9 to 12

There are one or two very old analyses in detail which are hardly reliable, and Dr. Ellis, of Toronto, has made investigations, still unpublished, in regard to the amount of tannin present, with a view to using the determination as a check on adulterants; but with these exceptions we are not aware of any other work upon the composition of this spice.

The authentic whole samples show that the percentage of water may be very variable, being at times as low as 2.90 per cent., and again as much as 10.67, which is high for so oily a substance. The ash, too, has rather wide extremes, varying from 5 to 13 per cent. The usual amount would not, however, be far from 5.50 to 6.50 per cent. Volatile oil falls in no case below the amount given by Dietsch, and serves as, perhaps, the best means of judging of the quality of the specimens. The extremes found in the pure specimens were 10.23 and 18.89 per cent., while but five out of the eleven ground specimens reached 10 per cent.

Other determinations do not seem especially characteristic. The extremes, which cannot be exceeded without casting suspicion, are:

	Per cent.
Water	11.00 to 2.75
Ash	13.00 to 5.00
Volatile oil	21.00 to 9.00
Fixed oil and resin	11.00 to 4.00
Crude fiber	10.00 to 6.00
Albuminoids	8.00 to 4.00

The determination of tannin, following the suggestions of Dr. Ellis, of Toronto, has been examined with results showing it to be of some value, but not as great as that of volatile oil. Our experience showed that it was as well to determine the matter oxidizable by permanganate, after removal of oil, &c., by Squibb's ether, as to make a more elaborate determination of tannin itself. In the best whole cloves from the importers the quercitannic acid equivalent of the oxidizable matter varied from 18.72 to 22.13 per cent., and in the stem reached 23.24 per cent. The determination will not, therefore, show the presence of stems in ground cloves. The amount fell also in one unidentified specimen of whole cloves to 11.70 per cent., but the quality of these buds was unknown. It is fair to assume, then, that good cloves should contain extractive oxidizable matter equivalent to 18 per cent. of quercitannic acid, or require an oxygen equivalent of about 4.50 per cent. for its reduction.

Of the 11 specimens of ground cloves examined, although none of them were of first quality, this tannin equivalent exceeded 18 in all but 3. The addition of stems and allspice would not be discovered, as both contain tannin in considerable amount. This determination is, then, in no way conclusive, but merely furnishes an indication which must be corroborated by other means. For the method of carrying it out reference must be made to our pages on analyses. As has been said, none of the ground specimens of cloves were first class, analyses showing that in only one case did the essential oil reach as high as 13.93 per cent., and although but 2 from Baltimore contained cheap foreign adulterants and none were sophisticated with allspice, all the specimens must have been made from a low grade of buds and many with the addition of large quantities of stems and spent cloves. The two cheapest specimens, 4873 and 4874, were, as has been said, terrible compounds of mineral coloring matter, leaving a dark ferruginous ash, corn meal, and hulls, evidence of which appears in the analyses from the low oil, 3.59 and 4.06 per cent., and the high crude fiber. The addition of so much organic matter low in ash conceals the presence of mineral coloring matter which is detected by its ferruginous appearance. In the ash of the whole buds, while there are at times some of a light reddish tinge, the color is distinctly or often dark green from the presence of manganese.

Our results show the universal and alarmingly poor quality of the commercial supply of ground cloves.

PIMENTO OR ALLSPICE.

Pimento is the fruit of *Pimenta officinalis*, an evergreen tree common in the West Indies. It is the only one of the common spices which had its origin in the New World. It is a small, dry, globular berry from two to three-tenths of an inch in diameter, having a short style and surrounded by four short thick sepals which often, however, have become rubbed off, leaving a scar-like ring. The berry has a woody shell, or pericarp, easily cut, and of dark, ferruginous brown, rugose by means of minute tubercles filled with essential oil. It is two-celled, each cell containing a single seed. The seed is less aromatic than the pericarp.

Under the microscope the outer layer of the pericarp, just beneath the epidermis, appears as a collection of very large brown parenchymatous cells filled with oil. The more interior layers consist of thick walled or stone cells loaded with resin, the most characteristic structure of the pimento, parenchyma cells, and smaller crystals of calcic oxalate which are not easily seen. The whole tissue is traversed, but not plentifully, by fibro-vascular bundles. The seeds contain much starch in minute grains and have a few oil cells. The embryo is large and spirally curved. The hulls of the seeds consist of a delicate epidermis and of large thin-walled cells with light or dark red contents, which are very characteristic and are called by Hassall the port-wine cells, which should be examined in water, and after treatment with chloral hydrate, the starch grains being made out in the water preparation and the remaining structure among the particles rendered transparent by the chloral hydrate. Most prominent among the latter under polarized light, which is here a great assistance, are the stone cells or thick walled cells partly grouped and partly separate, and often, with plain light, showing shreds of parenchyma adherent to them. The brown cells which contain the oil are made out with less distinctness, but most striking are the red or port-wine cells of the seed hull, which are seen scattered everywhere, and in color and form are very characteristic. Shreds of the embryo are also now and then seen.

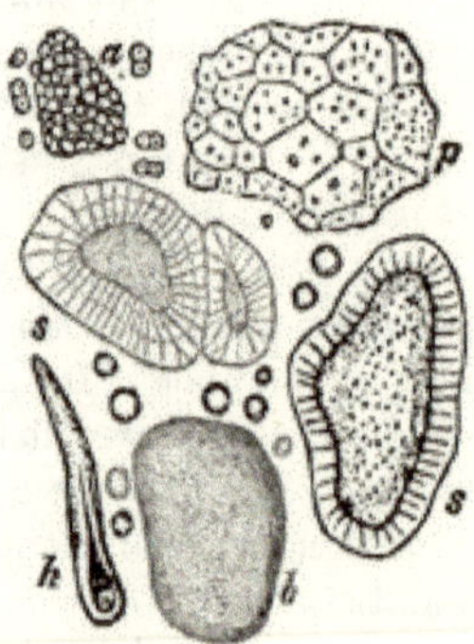

FIG. 13. Allspice powder. *a*, starch; *b*, port-wine cells; *h*, hairs; *s*, stone cells; *p*, parenchyma. ×240.

Schimper's diagramatic illustrations of this spice are here copied in Fig. 13, and serve as a slight aid to the recognition of the structures mentioned, but merely as suggestions, as nothing exactly corresponding to the drawings will be found in the ground powder.

Polarized light is a most important aid in examining this spice. It brings out strongly the stone-cells and ligneous tissue and differentiates therefrom the great mass of other matter. It also makes the oil cavities more distinct.

The adulteration of this spice does not often occur, owing to its cheapness. We have only found three cases, and those from Baltimore. In No. 4530 a substitution had been made for allspice, of which not a particle could be detected, of inferior cloves from which much of the volatile oil had been extracted, and Nos. 4877 and 4877, where yellow corn and mineral coloring matter were plentiful. In these instances chemical analysis confirmed the microscopic examination.

Abroad clove stems are said to be largely used as an adulterant. They differ from cloves, as has been already explained, in the presence of numerous stone-cells and fibro-vascular bundles, and in Canada peas and roasted corn have been found. The presence of these cheap diluents should be sought for, as in peppers, but they are less common in this spice.

CHEMICAL COMPOSITION OF ALLSPICE.

But little has been published in regard to the proximate principles of the pimento. The amount of volatile oil is said by Flückiger to be from 3 to 4½ per cent., while starch and much tannin are present in the berry. Dragendorff has also found a minute quantity of an alkaloid of the odor of coumarine. Hassall gives analyses, which are too old to be of any value, and quotes Pereira as an authority for the fact that the essential oil of pimento is made up of two distinct oils, which, of course, may be true in one sense but is hardly of value as a definite distinction, both for this spice and cloves, as has been already remarked.

As a matter of fact but little is known of this spice. We have examined seven samples with the results here given:

4500. Whole allspice.
4501. Ground allspice, guaranteed pure, Washington.
4518. Ground allspice, ground in Washington.
4525. Ground allspice, ground in Baltimore.
4530. Ground allspice, ground in Baltimore.
4534. Ground allspice, ground in Baltimore.
4538. Ground allspice, English brand.
4877. Ground allspice, best, cheap grade, Baltimore.
4878. Ground allspice, pure, cheap grade, Baltimore.

All the samples were ground by different firms except the last two.

Analyses of pimento, allspice.

Serial No.	Description.	Water.	Ash.	Volatile oil.	Fixed oil.	Undetermined.	Crude fiber.	Albuminoids.	Nitrogen.	Tannin equivalent.	O required.
4500	Whole	6.19	4.01	5.15	6.15	59.28	14.83	4.38	.70	10.97	**2.81**
4501	Commercial ground	5.51	2.93	2.93	6.10	58.24	17.95	5.34	.86	13.10	**3.36**
4518	......do	8.63	4.83	2.07	5.50	57.20	18.60	4.38	.70	9.31	**2.39**
4525	......do	8.82	4.91	3.32	6.18	57.90	13.45	5.42	.87	9.39	**2.40**
4530	......do	11.59	6.02	8.17	7.64	59.57	11.93	5.08	.81	18.72	**4.80**
4534	......do	7.31	3.45	3.16	6.92	58.58	16.55	4.03	.64	12.74	**3.27**
4538	......do	8.71	4.50	1.29	5.35	55.90	18.83	5.42	.87	10.92	**2.80**
4877	......do	7.98	5.52	2.80	3.77	56.86	18.98	4.38	.70	8.27	**2.12**
4878	......do	7.31	5.19	1.82	1.60	56.45	23.60	4.03	.67	4.32	**1.11**

In our analyses there is considerable variation among the samples. Taking the whole berry as the standard the others fall off very much in quality, as judged by the volatile oil, with the exception of number 4530, which, too, from its low fiber, high ash, and high volatile and fixed oil is suspicious, and proves to be a substitution of cloves and clove stems. The microscope has shown that this sample is inferior cloves, and it must therefore be rejected.

The amount of essential oil in our best sample exceeds Flückiger's highest, but on the ground specimens falls off sadly, 4538 and 4878 being almost worthless as far as this valuable ingredient goes, perhaps in the first case having been exhausted for the preparation of the oil, although the ash is but little reduced in amount, and in the latter being nothing but mixtures, as shown under the microscope.

The other determinations show no important variation in the constituents, and estimation of the volatile oil would perhaps be the only thing necessary in a chemical way in examining it, without it is desired to go into the determination of tannin, which is as serviceable a means of discriminating among allspices as was found to be the case with cloves.

In the same way our results show that good allspice contains oxidizable matter extracted by water after removal of oil, etc., by ether equivalent to from 9–11.0 per cent. of quercetannic acid, the amount being considerably smaller than is found in cloves. This determination points out at once that specimens 4530 and 4878 are abnormal, and that 4534 is suspicious. It may be made of value and must be carried out in the same way as with cloves. Of the eight ground specimens examined three were adulterated and one was suspicious, so that even of this cheap spice we can hardly expect a pure supply without some protection.

NUTMEG.

Nutmegs are the interior kernel of the fruit of *Myristica fragrans*, a tree growing in various parts of the East, but principally in the Banda Islands.

Flückiger and Hanbury describe in a most excellent way their characteristics as follows:

The fruit is a pendulous, globose drupe, about 2 inches in diameter, and not unlike a small round pear. It is marked by a furrow which passes around it, and by which at maturity its thick fleshy pericarp splits into two pieces, exhibiting in its interior a single seed, enveloped in a fleshy foliaceous mantle or arillus, of fine crimson hue, which is *mace*. The dark brown shining ovate seed is marked with impressions corresponding to the lobes of the arillus; and on one side, which is of paler hue and slightly flattened, a line indicating the raphe may be observed.

The bony testa does not find its way into European commerce, the so-called nutmeg being merely the kernel or nucleus of the seed. Nutmegs exhibit nearly the form of their outer shell with a corresponding diminition in size. The London dealers esteem them in proportion to their size, the largest, which are about one inch long by eight-tenths of an inch broad, and four of which will weigh an ounce, fetching the highest price. If not dressed with lime, they are of a grayish brown, smooth yet coarsely furrowed and veined longitudinally, marked on the flatter side with a shallow groove. A transverse section shows that the inner seed coat (endopleura) penetrates into the albumen in long narrow brown strips, reaching the center of the seed, thereby imparting the peculiar marbled appearance familiar in a cut nutmeg. * * *

The tissue of the seed can be cut with equal facility in any direction.

Of the microscopic structure they say:

The testa consists mainly of long, thin, radially arranged rigid cells, which are closely interlaced and do not exhibit any distinct cavities. The endopleura which forms the adhering coat of the kernel and penetrates into it, consists of soft walled, red brown tissue, with small scattered bundles of vessels. In the outer layers the endopleura exhibits small collapsed cells; but the tissue which fills the folds that dip into the interior consists of much larger cells

The tissue of the albumen is formed of soft-walled parenchyme, which is densely filled with conspicuous starch grains and with fat partly crystallized. Among the prismatic crystals of fat large, thick rhombic or six-sided tables may often be observed. With these are associated grains of albuminoid matter partly crystallized.

In carefully made preparations from the whole nutmeg the structure above described can be made out by care and patience. In the ground spice, however, of these characteristics only the interior parenchyma cells with their starchy contents can be seen when mounted in water, with the alternate use of common and polarized light. The fatty crystals we have not observed, and the fragments of the endopleura or red-brown tissue are characterized only by their color. In chloral hydrate the starch cells and grains are swollen, but the red-brown tissue is much more transparent, sufficiently so, in fact, to reveal any differences between it and any adulterant which might bear a resemblance. There are but few bundles of fibers to be found. The structure as a whole is so simple that the addition of any foreign material can be readily detected.

CHEMICAL COMPOSITION OF NUTMEG.

Analysis of these samples of nutmegs of the following origin have been made:

4512. Whole limed nutmeg, grocers.
4513. Ground limed nutmeg, grocers.
4546. Ground in Baltimore.

Serial No.	Water.	Ash.	Volatile oil.	Fixed oil or fat.	Starch, &c.	Crude fiber.	Albuminoids.	Total.	Nitrogen.
4512	6.08	3.27	2.84	34.37	36.98	11.30	5.16	100.00	.83
4513	4.19	2.22	3.97	37.30	40.12	6.78	5.42	100.00	.87
4546	6.40	3.15	2.90	30.98	41.77	9.55	5.25	100.00	.84

Flückiger states that the volatile oil of nutmegs amounts to between 3 and 8 per cent., and that it is of the nature of a terpene. The fat or fixed oil he places at one-fourth of the weight of the nutmeg, or 25.0 per cent., the principal constituents being starch and albuminoids. Beyond these facts gathered by this authority nothing of value seems to have been published in regard to the proximate percentage composition of nutmegs.

Our results with only three samples are fairly concordant. The volatile oil hardly reached the limit which has been mentioned. It is no doubt a variable quantity. The fixed oil or fat, on the other hand, far exceeds what was expected. Our more perfect methods of extraction may be partly the cause of these results, and it may be also due to a resinification of the portion of the volatile oil, thus reducing the percentage of this substance and increasing that of the fat.

The amount of starch and allied substances seems fairly constant, while that of albuminoids is rather lower than would be expected. The fiber is also low, but our methods of determining so called fiber are so indefinite that such determinations are of only of comparative value.

Without any actual trials it would seem that determinations of oil and fat, and perhaps of albuminoids and fiber, would serve well to detect foreign substances which would certainly modify in a striking way the normal relations of these proximate principles.

At present nutmegs are almost entirely sold whole and grated in the kitchen. Attempts at adulteration have, therefore, been few in number.

MACE.

The mantle or arillus of the nutmeg, a coat between the outside pericarp and the seed, is known as mace when separated and dried. The coat is not continuous, but is a net-work the form of which is recognizable in the dried spice.

Of its microscopic structure Flückiger and Hanbury say:

> The uniform, small-celled angular parenchyme is interrupted by numerous brown oil cells of larger size. The inner part of the tissue contains also thin brown vascular bundles. The cells of the epidermis on either side are colorless, thick walled, longitudinally extended, and covered with a peculiar cuticle of broad, flat ribbon-like cells, which cannot, however, be removed as a continuous film. The parenchyme is loaded with small granules, to which a red color is imparted by Millon's test (solution of mercurous nitrate) and an orange hue by iodine. The granules consequently consist of albuminous matter, and starch is altogether wanting.

This statement has been fully confirmed, and the presence of starch claimed by several writers disproved. Iodine produces a peculiar deep brown color approaching the black-blue given with starch, which, in connection with the granules, has given rise to the statements that starch is present.

In the ground powder of mace all the details of structure described by Flückiger are readily made out, especially in chloral hydrate preparations with polarized light, as the brown vascular bundles, the ribbon-like and epidermal cells all are polarizing substances, while the large mass of granular parenchyma cells are not. The ribbon-like cells are particularly interesting in the varied forms they assume. Adulterations can be readily detected.

CHEMICAL COMPOSITION OF MACE.

Flückiger and Hanbury found in mace 8.2 per cent. of essential oil and 24.5 per cent. of aromatic balsam or resinified aromatic oil but no fat; also 1.4 per cent. of uncrystallizable sugar and 1.8 of mucilage, or a body between that and starch, blued by iodine. The composition of mace they therefore find to be very different from that of nutmeg, contrary to the assertion of Hassall.

Three samples, which we have examined, gave the following results:

4508. Whole mace, guaranteed.
4509. Ground mace, guaranteed.
4535. Ground mace, Baltimore.
4879. Ground mace, Baltimore, low grade.

Analyses of mace.

Serial number.	Water.	Ash.	Volatile oil.	Resin.	Undetermined.	Crude fiber.	Albuminoids.	Total.	Nitrogen.
4508	5.67	4.10	4.04	27.50	41.17	8.93	4.55	100.00	.73
4509	4.86	2.65	8.66	29.08	35.50	4.48	6.13	100.00	.98
4535	10.47	2.20	8.68	23.33	34.68	6.88	5.08	100.00	.81
4879	8.90	3.23	5.39	35.09	28.01	12.20	7.18	100.00	1.15

The percentages of volatile oil agree with the determinations of Flückiger except in the sample ground from the whole nutmeg in our laboratory, which is deficient. The amount probably should always reach 8 per cent. in good nutmegs. The resin found averages rather higher than in Flückiger's specimen, but the presence of so large an amount is certainly very characteristic of this spice, as well of the nutmeg itself, and the presence of adulterants would, without doubt, unless skillfully provided for, be detected by the absence of more than 20 per cent. of this extractive matter.

No qualitative estimation was made of sugar and gum; they were detected qualitatively in small amounts, but from the determinations of fiber and albuminoids it is evident that a large amount of extractive matter not starch is present, and as Flückiger found only about 3 per cent. of substances soluble in alcohol and water and no starch, and as the non-nitrogenous material removed by acids amounts to 35 per cent., it is probably one of the numerous members of the cellulose group, related to gum or starch, which is contained in the parenchyma cells. In the absence of adulterated specimens it is difficult to say what methods of procedure should be taken for their detection; but aside from the microscopical examination, which would readily reveal most adulterants, the chemical characteristics seem to be so marked as to make the presence of any foreign substance evident in the results of analysis.

APPENDIX A.

BIBLIOGRAPHY OF THE LITERATURE OF SPICES AND CONDIMENTS.

The following bibliography consists of a list of such books and papers of any interest as have appeared, to my knowledge, within the last fifteen years. There has seemed to be no necessity for including anything published earlier than 1870, as the progress of investigation has left everything behind which was done before then. Blyth, however, in his work entitled "Foods, their Composition and analyses," gives lists of the ancient literature of the subject, which can be referred to by those who are interested in the historic rather than the analytical aspects of the subject. The works which were published before the date named and which are of interest to the analyst may also be found in a list given by Dr. Battershall in his recent publication.

GENERAL WORKS.

BATTERSHAL, J. P. [Adulteration of Food.] 1887.

BELL, JAMES. Food, Chemistry of. 1883. London.

BLYTH, A. WYNTER, 1876. A Dictionary of Hygiene, comprising the detection of adulteration. London, 1876.

BLYTH, A. W., 1882. Foods: their Composition and Analysis. Charles Griffin & Co., London.

CANADA, DOMINION OF, 1876 to date. Department of Inland Revenue. Reports on adulteration of food, being Supplement No. III to the report of. Ottawa, McLean, Roger & Co.

CHEVALLIER, A., 1878. Dictionnaire des altérations et falsifications des substances alimentaires, médicamenteuses et commerciales, avec l'indication des moyens pour les reconnaître. Paris, 5e éd., 1878, 2 Th.

DAMMER, OTTO. Illustrirtes Lexicon der Verfälschungen und Verunreinigungen der Nahrungs- und Genussmittel. Leipzig, 1886.

DIETZSCH, OSCAR, 1884. Die wichtigsten Nahrungsmittel und Getränke, deren Verunreinigungen- und Verfälschungen, u. s. w. Zürich, 1884, pp. 352, 8°.

ELSNER, FRITZ, 1882. Die Praxis des Nahrungsmittel-Chemikers. Hamburg-Leipzig, Leopold Voss, 1882, 8°, 216 ss.

FLÜCKIGER, FREDRICH A., & HANBURY, DANIEL. Pharmacographia. A History of the Principal Drugs, etc. 2d edit. London, Macmillan & Co., 1879, pp. 803.

FRANÇAISE, RÉPUBLIQUE, PRÉFECTURE DE POLICE. Documents sur les Falsifications des Matières alimentaires et sur les travaux du laboratoire municipal. 3 tomes. Paris, G. Masson.

HANAUSECK, T. F., 1884. Die Nahrungs- und Genussmittel aus dem Pflanzenreiche. Kassel, 1884, ss. 485.

HASSALL, ARTHUR HILL, 1876. Food. Its Adulterations and the Methods for their Detection. London, Longmans, Green & Co., 1876, 8°, 896 pp.

HILGER, ALBERT, 1885, Sept. Vereinbarungen betreffs der Untersuchungen und Beurteilung von Nahrungs- und Genussmittel sowie Gebrauchsgegenständen. Herausgegeben im Auftrage der freien Vereinigung bayrisher Vertreter der angewandten Chemie. Berlin, Julius Springer, 1885, pp. 283.

HILGER, A., and KAYSER, R., 1886. Bericht über die 4. Versammlung der freien Vereinigung Bayrischer Vertreter der angewandeten Chemie zu Nürnberg 7. und 8. Aug., 1885. Berlin, Julius Springer, 1886, 118 ss.

KAYSER, R., HOLZNER, VOGEL, HANS, PRIOR, E., LIST, E., and SENDTNER, R., '83. Sechs Vorträge auf dem Gebiete der Nahrungsmittel-Chemie. 1. Untersuchung von Nahrungs- und Genussmittel, sowie Verbrauchsgegenständen mit Bezugsnahme auf das Reichsgesetz von 14. Mai von R. Kayser. 2. Ueber Schultze'sche Tafeln von Holzner. 3. Ueber Milchuntersuchung und Milch-Control von Hans Vogel. 4. Untersuchung über den Hopfen. 5. Die Schwefelsäure in Wein, von E. List. 6. Die Untersuchung der Butter, von R. Sendtner. Würzburg, 1883.

KLENCKE, HERMANN, 1878. Illustrirtes Lexicon der Verfälschungen der Nahrungsmittel und Getränke. Leipzig, 1878.

KÖNIG, J., 188'.—Nahrungs- und Genussmittel, ihre Herstellung, Zusammensetzung und Beschaffenheit, ihre Verfälschungen und ihre Nachweisung. 2. Band. Berlin, Julius Springer, 1882, 8° ss. 620 and 351.

MASSACHUSETTS STATE BOARD OF HEALTH, LUNACY, AND CHARITY, 1879–188'. Supplements, containing the reports and papers on public health to the first, second, fourth, fifth, and sixth, etc., reports of.

MÖLLER, 1886. Mikroskopie der Nahrungs- und Genussmittel aus dem Pflanzenreich. 1886.

NEW YORK STATE BOARD OF HEALTH. Annual reports of 1880 to date. Albany, 8°.

SCHMIPFER, A. F. W., 1886. Anleitung zur mikroskopischen Untersuchung der Nahrungs- und Genussmittel. Jena, Gustav Fischer, 1886, ss. 140.

SOUBEIRAN, J. LEON, 1874. Nouveau dictionnaire des falsifications et des altérations des aliments, des médicaments, &c. Paris, 1874.

WALCHNER, J. H., 1875. Die Nahrungsmittel der Menschen, ihre Verfälschungen und Verunreinigung. Berlin, 1875, 8°, 324 ss.

WOOD, H. C., REMINGTON, J. P., and SADTLER, S. P., 1883, Jan. The Dispensatory the United States of America, 15. edition. Philadelphia, J. B. Lippincott & Co., 1883, 8°, pp. 1928.

GENERAL ARTICLES REFERRING TO SEVERAL OF THE SPICES.

BIECHELE, 1881. (Untersuchung gepulverte Gewürze.) (Extractive matter.) Abs. Zeit. anal. Chem. **20**, 229–298, from Correspbl. d. Verein anal. Chemikers, **2**, 70.

BORGMANN, E., 1883. Gewürzeuntersuchungen (Alcoholic Extracts.) Zeit. anal. Chem. **22**, 535–537.

FISCHER, FERD., 1880, Jan. (Zur Verfälschung, and Untersuchung von Nahrungs. und Genussmittel.) Title: Chem. Centbl. **11**, 221, from Poly. J. **235**, 140–150.

FISCHER, FERD., 1879, Dec. (Ausnutzung der Nahrungsmittel.) (1.) Nahrungsbedarf des Menschen, J. Ranke. (2.) Nahrwerth verschiedener Nahrungsmittel, Rubner. Title: Chem. Centrbl. **11**, 151 from Polyt. J. **234**, 486–489.

HILGER, A., 1879, 18 August. (Untersuchung der Nahrungs- und Genussmittel.) (Michl. Wurstwaaren, Essig und Gewürze.) Abs. Chem. Centbl. **10**, 40, from Arch. Pharm. [3] **13**, 428–433.

LAUBE, G., and ALDENDORF, H., 1879. Wider die Nahrungsfälscher. (Analyses of Spices.) Hannoversche Monatsschrift, 1879, 83. *Fide* König, J.

LEEDS, A. R., 1881. Upon the adulteration of food, drink, and drugs from the chemists' standpoint and upon the attitude of chemists in the matter of appointment of government analysts. Am. Chem. Soc. Jour. **3**, 60–62. Chem. News, **44**, 56.

SELL, EUGENE, 1883, 28 September. (Vortrag über Nahrungsmittel Chemiker und Nahrungsmittel Chemie. Abs. Chem. Centbl. **14**, 731–732.

WIGNER, G. W., and others, 1881. (Adulteration, Definition and Proposed Laws.) Analyst, **6**, 3.

WOLFF, C. H., 1881. Untersuchung gepulverter Gewürze. (Extractive matter.) Zeit. anal. Chem. **20**, 296-298, aus Corbl. d. Verein anal. Chemiker, 2, 91.

ARTICLES ON STARCHES.

DAFERT, F. W., 1885. Zur Kenntniss der Stärkearten. Landw. Jahrb. **14**, 831-838, **15**, 259-276; Abs. Bied. Centbl. **15**, 279-680.

MUTER, J., 1878. Organic Materia Medica. London, 1878.

NAGELLI, 1858. Die Stärkemehlkörner, 1858.

STRASSBURGER, EDUARD Das botanische Prakticum. Jena, 1884, ss. 666.

TRIPE, J. W., 1879, December. On the discrimination of starches by polarized light. Analyst **4**, 221-223.

WEISNER. Einleitung in die technischen Mikroskopie. Wien, 1867, 8°.

Vide also Hassall, Blyth, König, and others.

ARTICLES ON PARTICULAR SPICES.

PEPPER.

ANONYMOUS, 1883. (Test for pepper on aqueous iodine.) Pharm. Centralhalle, **24**, 510. Pharm. Centralhalle, **24**, 566. *Vide* Lenz, W. Zeit. Anal. Chem. **24**, 510.

BROWN, J. CAMPBELL, 1887, Feb. On Poivrette. Analyst, **12**, 23-25.

BROWN, J. CAMPBELL, 1887, March. Further note on Poivrette. Analyst, **12**, 47-48.

BROWN, J. CAMPBELL, 1887 On long pepper. Analyst, **12**, 67-70.

BROWN, J. CAMPBELL, 1887, April. Poivrette, Caution to Analysts. Analyst, **12**, 72.

BROWN, J. CAMPBELL, 1887, May. Another new pepper adulterant (Dhoura Corn). Analyst, **12**, 89.

DIEHL, C. LEWIS, 1881. Report to National Board of Health on adulteration of drugs (including pepper). Bull. Nat. Bd. Health, Supp. No. 6, Analyst, **6**, 50.

GEISSLER, E., 1883. (Untersuchung des Pfeffers.) Chem. Centbl. **15**, 70-71, aus Pharm. Central halle, **24**, 521-523.

HAGER, H. (Pfeffer Verfälschungen.) Heating with oxalic acid and water and determination of extract formed. *Vide* Lenz, Zeit. anal. Chem. **24**, 510.

HALENKE, A., 1886, Aug. 6. Referat über die zulässige Grenze von mineralischen Verunreinigungen des gemahlenen Pfeffers. Ber. 5te Vers. Bay. Vert. d angew. Chemie, 21-32.

HALENKE and MOSLINGER, 1885, Aug. 7 and 8. Ueber Pfefferverfälschung. Ber. Bayrischer Vert. angew. Chem., 1885, 104. Berlin, J. Springer, 1886.

HARVEY, SIDNEY, 1886, Nov. 10. Note upon the conversion of starch into glycerine by means of hydrochloric acid (in peppers). Analyst, **11**, 221-223. Abs. Am. J. of Pharm. **59**, 31-32.

HEISCH, C., 1886, Oct. Analyses of pepper. Analyst, **11**, 186-190. Abs. J. Chem. Soc., **52**, 312.

HILL, BOSTOCK, 1885. Note on a sample of adulterated pepper. Analyst, **10**, 122-123.

LENZ, W., 1884. Ein Beitrag zur chemischen Untersuchung von Pfefferpulver. Zeit. anal. Chem., **23**, 501-513.

MEYER, ARTHUR, 1883, Dec. (Die mikroskopische Untersuchung von Pflanzenpulver, speziell über den Nachweis von Buchweizenmehl in Pfefferpulver und über die Unterscheidung des Maismehls von dem Buchweizenmehl.) Abs. Chem. Centbl., **15**, 201. From Arch. Pharm. [3], **21**, 911-918.

NIEDERSTADT, 1886. (Piperin Bestimmung.) Rep. anal. Chim., **3**, 68.

RABOURDIN, H., 1884. De l'essai des poivres du commerce au point de vue de leur falsification par les grignons d'olive et les grabeaux. J. de Pharm. et de Chim., [5], **9**, 289-297. Abs. Pharm. Zeit., **29**, 375.

ROTTGER, DR., 1885, Aug. 7 and 8. Zur Untersuchung des Pfeffers. Ber. 4. Vers. Verein Bayrisch. Vertreter u. s. w., 1885, 97.

SCHUSCHING, H., 1885. (Pfeffer im Kleinhandel.) Abs. Chem. Centbl., **16**, 170. From Arch. f. Pharm.

WEIGMANN, H., 1886. Zur chemischen Untersuchung des Pfeffers. Abs. Deutsch. Chem. Zeitbl., 397. Title: Chem. Centbl. **17**, 744. From Rep. anal. Chem., **6**, 399-402.

MUSTARD.

HASSALL, A. H., 1877. (Ueber den Senf und dessen Verfälsshungen.) Title: Chem. Centlbl. **8**, 247, from Arch. Pharm. **3**, 10, 156.

LEEDS, ALBERT R., and EVERHART, EDGAR, 1882, July. (Eine Methode zur Analyse des Senfes.) Zeit. anal. Chem. **21**, 389-394. Abs. Chem. Centbl. **13**, 646-647.

PIESSE, CHARLES, and STANSELL, LIONEL, 1880. Analyses of black and white mustard. Analyst 5, 161-165. J. Pharm. et de Chimie [5] **3**, 252-254. Chem. Centbl. **12**, 374.

STEFFECK, H., 1887. Ein neues Fälschungmittel des weissen Senfes (*Sinapis alba*) Land. Vers. Sta. **33**, 411-415.

WALLER, E. and MARTIN, E. W., 1884. An examination of mustards manufactured, and sold in New York City. Analyst, **9**, 166-170.

CAYENNE

STROHMER, F., 1884. Die chemische Zusammensetzung and Prüfung des Paprikas Vorläufiger Mith. Chem. Centbl. [3], **15**, 577-580.

GINGER.

JONES, E. W. T., 1886, April. The amount of starch in ground ginger. Analyst, **11**, 75-77.

TRESH, 1883, May. (Die Bestandtheile des Ingwers.) Note, Chem. Centbl. **13**, 539, aus Pharm. J. and Trans. [3], **610**, 721. Arch. Pharm. [3], **20**, 372.

YOUNG, W. C., 1884. Some analyses of ginger. Analyst, **9**, 214-215.

CINNAMON AND CASSIA.

HEHNER, O., 1879. On the mineral constituents of cinnamon and cassia. Analyst **4**, 225-228.

HILGER, A., 1886.—Aschegehalt von Ceylon Zimmt. Arch. d. Pharm. **223**, 826. Abs. Zeit. anal. Chem., **25**, 592.

LOTZE, 1886. Sur l'essence de cannelle de Chine. J. Pharm. et de Chimie [5], **14**, 419-423.

APPENDIX B.

SOME OF THE LAWS RELATING TO ADULTERATION OF SPICES AND CONDIMENTS.

The following laws are the most valuable and important which have been recently enacted, and are of such character as to make their enforcement possible. There are a few other States having laws which are practically dead letters.

Some portions not relating to the subject of this part of the Bulletin are omitted.*

LEGISLATION.

The New York State general law, of 1881, for the prevention of the adultera tion of food and drugs is as follows:

SECTION 1. No person shall, within this State, manufacture, have, offer for sale, or sell any article of food or drugs which is adulterated within the meaning of this act, and any person violating this provision shall be deemed guilty of a misdemeanor, and upon conviction thereof shall be punished by fine not exceeding fifty dollars for the first offense, and not exceeding one hundred dollars for each subsequent offense.

2. The term "food," as used in this act, shall include every article used for food or drink by man. The term "drug," as used in this act, shall include all medicines for internal and external use.

3. An article shall be deemed to be adulterated within the meaning of this act:

a. In the case of drugs.

(1) If, when sold under or by a name recognized in the United States Pharmacopœia, it differs from the standard of strength, quality, or purity laid down therein.

(2) If, when sold under or by a name not recognized in the United States Pharmacopœia, but which is found in some other pharmacopœia or other standard work on materia medica, it differs materially from the standard of strength, quality, or purity laid down in such work.

(3) If its strength or purity fall below the professed standard under which it is sold.

b. In the case of food or drink.

(1) If any substance or substances has or have been mixed with it so as to reduce or lower or injuriously affect its quality or strength.

(2) If any inferior or cheaper substance or substances have been substituted wholly or in part for the article.

(3) If any valuable constituent of the article has been wholly or in part abstracted.

(4) If it be an imitation of, or be sold under the name of, another article.

(5) If it consists wholly or in part of a diseased or decomposed, or putrid or rotten, animal or vegetable substance, whether manufactured or not, or, in te case of milk, if it is the produce of a diseased animal.

* I am indebted to the secretaries of the various States and Dr. Battershall for the material here collected.

(6) If it be colored, or coated, or polished, or powdered, whereby damage is concealed, or it is made to appear better than it really is, or of greater value.

(7) If it contain any added poisonous ingredient, or any ingredient which may render such article injurious to the health of the person consuming it: *Provided,* That the State board of health may, with the approval of the governor, from time to time declare certain articles or preparations to be exempt from the provisions of this act: *And provided further,* That the provisions of this act shall not apply to mixtures or compounds recognized as ordinary articles of food, provided that the same are not injurious to health and that the articles are distinctly labeled as a mixture, stating the components of the mixture.

4. It shall be the duty of the State board of health to prepare and publish from time to time lists of the articles, mixtures, or compounds declared to be exempt from the provisions of this act in accordance with the preceding section. The State board of health shall also from time to time fix the limits of variability permissible in any article of food or drug or compound, the standard of which is not established by any national pharmacopœia.

5. The State board of health shall take cognizance of the interests of the public health as it relates to the sale of food and drugs and the adulteration of the same, and make all necessary investigations and inquiries relating thereto. It shall also have the supervision of the appointment of public analysts and chemists, and upon its recommendation whenever it shall deem any such officers incompetent the appointment of any and every such officer shall be revoked and be held to be void and of no effect. Within thirty days after the passage of this act the State board of health shall meet and adopt such measures as may seem necessary to facilitate the enforcement of this act, and prepare rules and regulations with regard to the proper methods of collecting and examining articles of food or drugs, and for the appointment of the necessary inspectors and analysts; and the State board of health shall be authorized to expend, in addition to all sums already appropriated for said board, an amount not exceeding ten thousand dollars for the purpose of carrying out the provisions of this act. And the sum of ten thousand dollars is hereby appropriated, out of any moneys in the treasury not otherwise appropriated, for the purposes in this section provided.

6. Every person selling or offering or exposing any article of food or drugs for sale, or delivering any article to purchasers, shall be bound to serve or supply any public analyst or other agent of the State or local board of health appointed under this act, who shall apply to him for that purpose, and on his tendering the value of the same, with a sample sufficient for the purpose of analysis of any article which is included in this act, and which is in the possession of the person selling, under a penalty not exceeding $50 for a first offense and $100 for a second and subsequent offense.

7. Any violation of the provisions of this act shall be treated and punished as a misdemeanor; and whoever shall impede, obstruct, hinder, or otherwise prevent any analyst, inspector, or prosecuting officer in the performance of his duty shall be guilty of a misdemeanor, and shall be liable to indictment and punishment therefor.

8. Any acts or parts of acts inconsistent with the provisions of this act are hereby repealed.

9. All the regulations and declarations of the State board of health made under this act from time to time, and promulgated, shall be printed in the statutes at large.

10. This act shall take effect at the expiration of ninety days after it shall become a law.

Amendment of April 29, 1885.

SECTION 1. The title of chapter 407 of the laws of 1881, entitled "An act to prevent the adulteration of food and drugs," is hereby amended to read as follows: "An act to prevent the adulteration of food, drugs, and spirituous, fermented, or malt liquors in the State of New York."

* * * * * * *

3. Section 2 is hereby amended to read as follows:

"2. The term food as used in this act shall include every article of food or drink by man, including teas, coffees, and spirituous, fermented, and malt liquors. The term drug as used in this act shall include all medicines for internal or external use."

* * * * * * *

5. Section 5 is hereby amended to read as follows:

"5. The State board of health shall take cognizance of the interests of the public health as relates to the sale of food, drugs, spirituous, fermented, and malt liquors, and the adulteration thereof, and make all necessary inquiries relating thereto. It shall have the supervision of the appointment of public analysts and chemists, and upon its recommendation, whenever it shall deem any such officers incompetent, the appointment of any and every such officer shall be revoked and be held to be void and of no effect. Within thirty days after the passage of this act, and from time to time thereafter as it may deem expedient, the said board of health shall meet and adopt such measures, not provided for by this act, as may seem necessary to facilitate the enforcement of this act, and for the purpose of making an examination or analysis of spirituous, fermented, or malt liquors sold or exposed for sale in any store or place of business not herein otherwise provided for, and prepare rules and regulations with regard to the proper methods of collecting and examining articles of food, drugs, spirituous, fermented, or malt liquors, and for the appointment of the necessary inspectors and analysts. The said board shall at least once in the calendar year cause samples to be procured, in public market or otherwise, of the spirituous, fermented, or malt liquors distilled, brewed, manufactured, or offered for sale in each and every brewery or distillery located in this State, and a test, sample, or analysis thereof to be made by a chemist or analyist duly appointed by said board of health. The samples shall be kept in vessels and in a condition necessary and adequate to obtain a proper test and analysis of the liquors contained therein. The vessels containing such samples shall be properly labeled and numbered by the secretary of said board of health, who shall also prepare and keep an accurate and proper list of the names of the distillers, brewers, or venders, and opposite each name shall appear the number which is written or printed upon the label attached to the vessel containing the sample of the liquor manufactured, brewed, distilled, or sold. Such lists, numbers, and labels shall be exclusively for the information of the said board of health, and shall not be disclosed or published unless upon discovery of some deleterious substance prior to the completion of the analysis, except when required in evidence in a court of justice. The samples when listed and numbered shall be delivered to the chemist, analyst, or other officer of said board of health, and shall be designated and known to such chemist, analyst, or officer only by its number, and by no other mark or designation. The result of the analysis or investigation shall thereupon, and within a convenient time, be reported by the officer conducting the same to the secretary of said State board of health, setting forth explicitly the nature of any deleterious substance, compound, or adulteration which may be detrimental to public health and which has been found upon analysis in such samples, and stating the number of the samples in which said substance was found. Upon such examination or analysis the brewer, distiller, or vendor in whose sample of spirituous, fermented, or malt liquor such deleterious substances, compounds, or adulterations shall be found, shall be deemed to have violated the provisions of this act, and shall be punishable as prescribed in section 7 of this act."

* * * * * * *

7. Section 7 of said chapter 407 of the laws of 1881 is hereby amended to read as follows:

"7. Upon discovering that any person has violated any of the provisions of this act, the State board of health shall immediately communicate the facts to the district attorney of the county in which the person accused of such violation resides or carries on business, and the said district attorney, upon receiving such communication or notification, shall forthwith commence proceeding for indictment and trial of the accused as prescribed by law in cases of misdemeanor."

8. The State board of health shall be authorized to expend, in addition to the sums already appropriated for said board, an amount not exceeding $3,000, for the purpose of carrying out the provisions of this act, in relation to spirituous, fermented, or malt liquors. And the sum of $3,000 is hereby appropriated out of any moneys in the treasury not otherwise appropriated and expended for the purposes of this act.

9. This act shall take effect immediately.

The New Jersey general law is the same as that of New York.

Following are the rules of the New Jersey board of health for its inspectors and analysts:

DUTIES OF INSPECTORS.

1. The inspector is to buy samples of food or drugs, and to seal each sample in the presence of a witness.

2. The inspector must affix to each sample a label bearing a number, his initials, and the date of purchase.

3. Under no circumstance is the inspector to inform the analyst as to the source of the sample before the analysis shall have been completed and formally reported to the president or secretary of the state board of health.

4. Inspectors are to keep a record of each sample as follows:
   (1) Number of sample.
   (2) Date and time of purchase.
   (3) Name of witness to sealing.
   (4) Name and address of seller.
   (5) Name and address of producer, manufacturer, or wholesaler, when known, with marks on original package.
   (6) Name of analyst and date of sending.
   (7) How sent to analyst.

5. If the seller desires a portion of the sample, the inspector is to deliver it under seal. The duplicate sample left with seller should have a label containing the same marks as are affixed to the portion taken by the inspector.

6. The inspector is to deliver the sample to the analyst, taking his receipt for the same, or he may send it by registered mail, express, or special messenger.

DUTIES OF THE ANALYSTS.

1. The analyst is to analyze the samples immediately upon receipt thereof.

2. Samples, with the exception of milk and similar perishable articles, are to be divided by the analyst and a portion sealed up, and a copy of the original label affixed. These duplicates are to be sent to the secretary of the state board of health at the end of each month, and to be retained by him until demanded for another analysis, as provided for in section 3 of these rules.

3. Should the result obtained by any analyst be disputed in any case, an appeal may be made to the State board of health, through its secretary, by the defendant or person selling the sample, or his attorney, and said secretary shall then require another member of the committee of public analysts to repeat the analysis, using the duplicate sample for such purpose. But when an appeal shall be made, a sum of money sufficient to cover the expenses of the second analysis shall be deposited with the president of the state board of health, which sum shall be paid over to the analyst designated by the president and secretary of the board to perform the second analysis, in case the analysis shall be found to agree with the first in all essential particulars.

4 In the case of all articles having a standard of purity fixed by any of the laws of the State, the certificate of the analyst should show the relation of the article in question to that standard.

5. Where standards of strength, purity, or quality are not fixed by law, the committee of analysts shall present to the State board of health such standard as in their judgment should be fixed.

6. Each analyst should keep a record book, in which should be entered notes, as follows:

(1) From whom the sample is received.

(2) Date, time, and manner in which the sample was received.

(3) Marks on package, sealed or not.

(4) Results of analysis in detail.

This record should be produced at each meeting of the committee.

7. At the completion of the analysis a certificate in the form given below should be forwarded to the person from whom the sample was received, and a duplicate copy sent to the State board of health.

CERTIFICATE.

To whom it may concern:

I, ——, a member of the committee of public analysts, appointed by the State board of health of New Jersey under provisions of an act entitled "An act to prevent the adulteration of food and drugs," approved March 25, 1881, do hereby certify that I received from ——, on the —— day of ——, 188–, a sample of ——, sealed as required by the rules of said board, and bearing the following words, to wit:——

I carefully mixed said samples and have analyzed the same, and hereby certify and declare the results of my analyses to be as follows: ——.

[Signature.] —— ——.

EXCEPTIONS.

The following exceptions are adopted:

Mustard.—Compounds of mustard with rice flour, starch, or flour may be sold if each package is marked "Compound Mustard," and if not more than 25 per cent. of such substance is added to the mustard.

Coffee.—Compounds of coffee with chicory, rye, wheat, or other cereals, may be sold if the package is marked "A Mixture," and if the label states the per cent. of coffee contained in said mixture.

Oleomargarine and other imitation dairy products may be sold if each package is marked with the name of the substance, and in all respects fulfils the terms of the special law as to these.

Sirups.—When mixed with glucose, sirup may be sold if the package is marked "A Mixture."

The following are the statutes of the State of Massachusetts relating to the adulteration of food and drugs:

General Laws relating to Adulteration.

FOOD AND DRUGS.

Section 1. No person shall, within this Commonwealth, manufacture for sale, offer for sale, or sell any drug or article of food which is adulterated within the meaning of this act.

2. The term "drug" as used in this act shall include all medicines for internal or external use, antiseptics, disinfectants, and cosmetics. The term "food" as used herein shall include all articles used for food or drink by man.

3. An article shall be deemed to be adulterated within the meaning of this act—

(*a*) *In the case of drugs.*—(1) If, when sold under or by a name recognized in the United States Pharmacopœia, it differs from the standard of strength, quality, or purity laid down therein, unless the order calls for an article inferior to such standard, or unless such difference is made known or so appears to the purchaser at the time of such sale; (2) if, when sold under or by a name not recognized in the United States Pharmacopœia, but which is found in some other pharmacopœia, or other standard work on *materia medica*, it differs materially from the standard of strength, quality, or purity laid down in such work; (3) if its strength or purity falls below the professed standard under which it is sold.

(*b*) *In the case of food.*—(1) If any substance or substances have been mixed with it so as to reduce, or lower, or injuriously affect its quality or strength; (2) if any inferior or cheaper substance or substances have been substituted wholly or in part for it; (3) if any valuable constituent has been wholly or in part abstracted from it; (4) if it is an imitation of or is sold under the name of another article; (5) if it consists wholly or in part of a diseased, decomposed, putrid, or rotten animal or vegetable substance, whether manufactured or not, or in the case of milk, if it is the produce of a diseased animal; (6) if it is colored, coated, polished, or powdered, whereby damage is concealed, or if it is made to appear better or of greater value than it really is; (7) if it contains any added or poisonous ingredient, or any ingredient which may render it injurious to the health of a person consuming it.

4. The provisions of this act shall not apply to mixtures or compounds recognized as ordinary articles of food or drinks, provided that the same are not injurious to health and are distinctly labeled as mixtures or compounds. And no prosecutions shall at any time be maintained under the said act concerning any drug the standard of strength or purity whereof has been raised since the issue of the last edition of the United States Pharmacopœia, unless and until such change of standard has been published throughout the Commonwealth.

5. The State board of health, lunacy, and charity shall take cognizance of the interests of the public health relating to the sale of drugs and food and the adulteration of the same, and shall make all necessary investigations and inquiries in reference thereto, and for these purposes may appoint inspectors, analysts, and chemists, who shall be subject to its supervision and removal.

Within thirty days after the passage of this act the said board shall adopt such measures as it may deem necessary to facilitate the enforcement hereof, and shall prepare rules and regulations with regard to the proper methods of collecting and examining drugs and articles of food. Said board may expend annually an amount not exceeding ten thousand dollars for the purpose of carrying out the provisions of this act: *Provided, however,* That not less than three-fifths of the said amount shall be annually expended for the enforcement of the laws against the adulteration of milk and milk products.

6. Every person offering or exposing for sale, or delivering to a purchaser, any drug or article of food included in the provisions of this act, shall furnish to any analyst or other officer or agent appointed hereunder, who shall apply to him for the purpose and shall tender him the value of the same, a sample sufficient for the purpose of the analysis of any such drug or article of food which is in his possession.

7. Whoever hinders, obstructs, or in any way interferes with any inspector, analyst, or other officer appointed hereunder, in the performance of his duty, and whoever violates any of the provisions of this act, shall be punished by a fine not exceeding fifty dollars for the first offense, and not exceeding one hundred dollars for each subsequent offense.

8. The State board of health, lunacy, and charity shall report annually to the legislature the number of prosecutions made under said chapter, and an itemized account of all money expended in carrying out the provisions thereof.

9. An inspector appointed under the provisions of said chapter two hundred and sixty-three of the acts of the year eighteen hundred and eighty-two shall have the same powers and authority conferred upon a city or town inspector by section two of chapter fifty-seven of the public statutes.

10. Nothing contained in chapter two hundred and sixty-three of the acts of the year eighteen hundred and eighty-two shall be in any way construed as repealing or amending anything contained in chapter fifty-seven of the public statutes.

11. Before commencing the analysis of any sample, the person making the same shall reserve a portion which shall be sealed; and in case of a complaint against any person the reserved portion of the sample alleged to be adulterated shall upon application be delivered to the defendant or his attorney.

12. Whoever knowingly sells any kind of diseased, corrupted, or unwholesome provisions, whether for meat or drink, without making the same fully known to the buyer, shall be punished by imprisonment in the jail not exceeding six months, or by fine not exceeding two hundred dollars.

13. Whoever fraudulently adulterates, for the purpose of sale, bread or any other substance intended for food, with any substance injurious to health, or knowingly barters, gives away, sells, or has in possession with intent to sell, any substance intended for food, which has been adulterated with any substance injurious to health, shall be punished by imprisonment in the jail not exceeding one year, or by fine not exceeding three hundred dollars; and the articles so adulterated shall be forfeited and destroyed under the direction of the court.

14. Whoever adulterates, for the purpose of sale, any liquors used or intended for drink, with Indian cockle, vitriol, grains of paradise, opium, alum, capsicum, copperas, laurel-water, logwood, Brazil wood, cochineal, sugar of lead, or any other substance which is poisonous or injurious to health, and whoever knowingly sells any such liquor so adulterated, shall be punished by imprisonment in the State prison not exceeding three years; and the articles so adulterated shall be forfeited.

15. Whoever fraudulently adulterates, for the purpose of sale, any drug or medicine, or sells any fraudulently adulterated drug or medicine, knowing the same to be adulterated, shall be punished by imprisonment in the jail not exceeding one year or by fine not exceeding four hundred dollars; and such adulterated drugs and medicines shall be forfeited and destroyed under the direction of the court.

16. Whoever sells arsenic, strychnine, corrosive sublimate, or prussic acid, without the written prescription of a physician, shall keep a record of the date of such sale, the name of the article, the amount thereof sold, and the name of the person or persons to whom delivered; and for each neglect shall forfeit a sum not exceeding fifty dollars. Whoever purchases deadly poisons as aforesaid, and gives a false or fictitious name to the vendor, shall be punished by fine not exceeding fifty dollars.

CHAP. 171.—AN ACT concerning the adulteration of food and drugs.

Be it enacted, etc., as follows:

Section two of chapter two hundred and sixty-three of the acts of the year eighteen hundred and eighty-two is hereby amended so as to read as follows: The term "drug" as used in this act shall include all medicines for internal or external use, antiseptics, disinfectants, and cosmetics. The term "food" as used herein shall include confectionery, condiments, and all articles used for food or drink by man.—Approved April 29, 1886.

RULES AND REGULATIONS OF THE STATE BOARD OF HEALTH, LUNACY, AND CHARITY OF MASSACHUSETTS RELATIVE TO THE INSPECTION AND ANALYSIS OF FOOD AND DRUGS.

1. The state board of health, lunacy, and charity shall appoint analysts and inspectors, as provided in section 5 of chapter 263, acts of 1882.

2. It shall be the duty of the inspectors to procure samples of drugs and articles of food at such times and places as the health officer shall direct, in the manner provided in section 6 of chapter 263 of the acts of 1882, and in section 3 of chapter 289 of the acts of 1884, and in all acts amendatory of said provisions.

3. Under the direction of the health officer, one of the inspectors shall, for the identification of samples, affix a number to each sample of food or drugs obtained by him, beginning with number one, and taking every alternate or odd number thereafter, without limit: and the other inspector shall use and affix each alternate or even number, beginning with number two, and following such form of numbering, without limit, also, as far as may be directed. Under no circumstances shall an inspector convey any information to an analyst as to the source from which any sample was obtained.

4. The inspectors shall keep records of each sample, each record to include the following items:

(*a*) The inspector's number.

(*b*) The date of purchase or receipt of sample.

(*c*) The character of the sample.

(*d*) The name of the vender.

(*e*) The name of the city or town and street and number where the sample is obtained, and in the case of a licensed milk peddler, the number of his license.

(*f*) As far as possible, the names of manufacturers, producers, or wholesalers, with marks, brands, or labels stamped or printed upon goods.

5. It shall be the duty of the analysts so appointed to determine, under the direction of the health officer, by proper examination and analysis, whether articles of food and drugs, manufactured for sale, offered for sale, or sold within this Commonwealth, are adulterated within the meaning of chapter 263 of the acts and resolves passed by the general court of Massachusetts in 1882, and all acts amendatory thereof, adulteration being defined as follows, viz:

In the case of drugs, (1) If sold under or by a name recognized in the United States Pharmacopœia, it differs from the standard of strength, quality, or purity laid down therein, unless the order calls for an article inferior to such standard, or unless such difference is made known or so appears to the purchaser at the time of such sale. (2) If, when sold under or by a name not recognized in the United States Pharmacopœia, but which is found in some other pharmacopœia or standard work on materia medica, it differs materially from the standard of strength, quality, or purity laid down in such work. (3) If its strength or purity falls below the professed standard under which it is sold.

In the case of food, (1) If any substance or substances have been mixed with it, so as to reduce or lower or injuriously affect its quality or strength. (2) If any inferior or cheaper substance or substances have been substituted, wholly or in part, for it. (3) If any valuable constituent has been wholly or in part abstracted from it. (4) If it is an imitation of or is sold under the name of another article. (5) If it consists wholly or in part of a diseased, decomposed, putrid, or rotten animal or vegetable substance, whether manufactured or not, or in the case of milk, if it is the produce of a diseased animal. (6) If it is colored, coated, polished, or powdered, whereby damage is concealed, or if it is made to appear of better or of greater value than it really is. (7) If it contains any added poisonous ingredient, or any ingredient which may render it injurious to the health of the person consuming it.

6. It shall also be the duty of the analysts to receive such specimens of food and drugs for analysis as may be delivered to them by the health officer, or by the inspectors, and to examine the same. To avoid, as far as possible, all suggestion or danger of specimens having been tampered with, each analyst shall keep each specimen in his possession in a suitable and secure place, labeled in such a manner as to prevent any person from having access to the same, without the knowledge and presence of the analyst.

Analyses of perishable articles should be made promptly after they are received.

7. An analyst shall give no information, under any circumstances, regarding the result of any analysis to any person except to the health officer of the board, prior to any trial in court in reference to such analysis.

The analysts shall carefully avoid any error regarding the inspector's number attached to each sample, and shall report the results of their work in detail to the health officer.

In the case of all articles having a numerical standard provided by statute, the result of the analysis should show their relation to such standard.

8. Before beginning the analysis of any sample, the analyst shall reserve a portion, which shall be sealed, and in the event of finding the portion analyzed to be adulterated, he shall preserve the sealed portion, so that in case of a complaint against any person the last-named portion may, on application, be delivered by the health officer to the defendant or to his attorney.

9. Each analyst shall present to the health officer on the Thursday before the first Saturday of each month, a summary of the analyses made by him during the previous month.

Each analyst shall also present, on or before the first of January of each year, an annual report of the work done for the year ending on the 30th of September preceding.

10. The health officer shall have charge of the reports of analyses, and shall cause cases founded on such reports to be submitted to the courts for prosecution.

In each case of a retailer, and of every dealer not a manufacturer or producer, he may, if the party has not been previously complained of in court, issue a notice or warning of any violation of the law relative to the adulteration of food and drugs, and of the offender's liability to prosecution on a repetition of the sale.

11. Should the result obtained by any analyst be questioned in any given case, another analyst shall repeat the analysis, unless otherwise instructed by the board, provided a sufficient sum to meet the expense of the analysis be deposited with the health officer by any interested party feeling aggrieved, which sum will not be returned unless the second analysis fails to confirm the first in essential particulars.

12. Any appeal from the decision of an analyst shall be filed with the health officer, who shall report it, and any matter in controversy, to the board, giving his judgment thereon, and the board shall supervise and control the action of its officers, in executing the law.

13. Where standards of strength, quality, or purity are not fixed by the act, the analysts shall present to the health officer such standard as in their judgment should be fixed, and the health officer shall report the same to the board for its action. The standards set by the British Society of Public Analysts will be followed as nearly as practicable, until otherwise ordered.

14. Whenever a drug or preparation not described in a National Pharmacopœia or other standard work on materia medica, shall be manufactured, offered for sale, or used in this State, the standard of such drug, and the standard and proportion of the ingredients of such preparation, and the range of variability from such standard or standards shall be ascertained by the analysts, who shall report the same through the health officer to the board.

15. The analysts shall occupy such time in the performance of their respective duties as a reasonable compliance with the terms of the statute shall require, and shall be present one hour of each day at such time of the day and at such place as shall be designated by the committee on health of the board, to meet the convenience of interested parties and the public.

16. The compensation of the analyst of articles of food shall be at the rate of $1,500 per annum, and that of the analyst of drugs shall be at the rate of $1,000.

That of the analyst of milk for the ten eastern counties of the Commonwealth shall be at the rate of $800 per annum, and that of the analyst of the four western counties shall be at the rate of $500 per annum.

The compensation of each inspector shall be at the rate of $1,000 per annum.

The laws of Michigan are as follows:

ADULTERATION OF FOODS, DRINKS, DRUGS, OR MEDICINES.

208. (7727.) SEC. 2. If any person shall fraudulently adulterate, for the purpose of sale, any substance intended for food, or any wine, spirits, malt liquor, or other liquor intended for drinking, he shall be punished by imprisonment in the county jail not more than one year, or by fine not exceeding three hundred dollars, and the article so adulterated shall be forfeited and destroyed.—§9317.

209. (7728.) SEC. 3. If any person shall fraudulently adulterate, for the purpose of sale, any drug or medicine, in such manner as to render the same injurious to health, he shall be punished by imprisonment in the county jail not more than one year, or by fine not exceeding four hundred dollars, and such adulterated drugs and medicines shall be forfeited and destroyed.—§9318.

ADULTERATION OF FOODS, DRINKS, AND MEDICINES, AND SALE THEREOF WHEN ADULTERATED.

Act No. 254, laws of 1881, entitled "An Act to prevent and punish the adulteration of articles of food, drink, and medicine, and the sale thereof when adulterated."

210. SECTION 1. *The People of the State of Michigan enact*, That no person shall mix, color, stain, or powder, or order or permit any other person to mix, color, stain, or powder any article of food with any ingredient or material so as to render the article injurious to health, with the intent that the same may be sold; and no person shall knowingly sell or offer for sale any such article so mixed, colored, stained, or powdered.—§9324.

211. SEC. 2. No person shall, except for the purpose of compounding in the necessary preparation of medicine, mix, color, stain, or powder, or order or permit any other person to mix, color, stain, or powder, any drug or medicine with any ingredient or ingredients or materials so as to affect injuriously the quality or potency of such drug or medicine, with intent to sell the same, or shall sell or offer for sale any such drug or medicine so mixed, colored, stained, or powdered.—§9325.

212. SEC. 3. No person shall mix, color, stain, or powder any article of food, drink, or medicine, or any article which enters into the composition of food, drink, or medicine, with any other ingredient or material, whether injurious to health or not, for the purpose of gain or profit, or sell or offer the same for sale, or order or permit any other person to sell or offer for sale any article so mixed, colored, stained, and powdered, unless the same be so manufactured, used, or sold, or offered for sale under its true and appropriate name, and notice that the same is mixed or impure is marked, printed, or stamped upon each package, roll, parcel, or vessel containing the same, so as to be and remain at all times readily visible, or unless the person purchasing the same is fully informed by the seller of the true name and ingredients (if other than such as are known by the common name thereof) of such article of food, drink, or medicine at the time of making sale thereof or offering to sell the same.—§9326.

213. SEC. 4. No person shall mix any glucose or grape sugar with syrup, honey, or sugar, intended for human food, or any oleomargarine, suine, beef fat, lard, or any other foreign substance, with any butter or cheese intended for human food, or shall mix or mingle any glucose or grape sugar or oleomargarine with any article of food, without distinctly marking, stamping, or labeling the article, or the package containing the same, with the true and appropriate name of such article, and the percentage in which glucose or grape sugar, oleomargarine, or suine, enter into its composition; nor shall any person sell, or offer for sale, or order or permit to be sold, or offered for sale, any such food into the composition of which glucose, or grape sugar, or oleomargarine, or suine has entered, without at the same time informing the buyer of the fact, and the proportions in which such glucose or grape sugar, oleomargarine, or suine has entered into its composition.—§9327.

214. Sec. 5. Any person convicted of violating any provision of any of the forego ing sections of this act shall be fined not more than fifty dollars or imprisoned in the county jail not exceeding three months.—§9328.

215. Sec. 6. It is hereby made the duty of the prosecuting attorneys of this State to appear for the people and to attend to the prosecution of all complaints under this act in all the courts in their respective counties.—§9329.

216. Sec. 7. All acts and parts of acts inconsistent with the provisions of this act are hereby repealed.—§9330.

The Canadian law is as follows, in addition to which there is an elaborate act respecting the inspection of staple articles of Canadian produce:

Chapter 107.—An Act respecting the adulteration of food, drugs, and agricultural fertilizers.

Her Majesty, by and with the advice and consent of the Senate and House of Commons of Canada, enacts as follows:

SHORT TITLE.

1. This act may be cited as "*The adulteration act.*"—48–49 V., c. 67, s. 1.

INTERPRETATION.

2. In this act, unless the context otherwise requires—

(*a*) The expression "food" includes every article used for food or drink by man or by cattle.

(*b*) The expression "drug" includes all medicines for internal or external use for man or for cattle.

(*c*) The expression "agricultural fertilizer" means and includes every substance imported, manufactured, prepared, or disposed of for fertilizing or manuring purposes which is sold at more than ten dollars per ton and which contains phosphoric acid or ammonia or its equivalent of nitrogen.

(*d*) The expression "officer" means any officer of inland revenue or any person authorized under this act or "*the fertilizers act*" to procure samples of articles of food, drugs, or agricultural fertilizers and to submit them for analysis.

(*e*) Food shall be deemed to be "adulterated" within the meaning of this act—

(1) If any substance has been mixed with it so as to reduce or lower or injuriously affect its quality or strength.

(2) If any inferior or cheaper substance has been substituted, wholly or in part, for the article.

(3) If any valuable constituent of the article has been wholly or in part abstracted.

(4) If it is an imitation of, or is sold under the name of, another article.

(5) If it consists wholly or in part of a diseased or decomposed or putrid or rotten animal or vegetable substance, whether manufactured or not, or, in the case of milk or butter, if it is the produce of a diseased animal or of an animal fed upon unwholesome food.

(6) If it contains any added poisonous ingredient or any ingredient which may render such an article injurious to the health of a person consuming it.

(*f*) Every drug shall be deemed to be "adulterated" within the meaning of this act—

(1) If, when sold or offered or exposed for sale under or by a name recognized in the British or United States pharmacopœia, it differs from the standard of strength, quality, or purity laid down therein.

(2) If, when sold or offered or exposed for sale under or by a name not recognized in the British or United States pharmacopœia, but which is found in some other generally recognized pharmacopœia or other standard work on *materia medica*, it differs from the standard of strength, quality, or purity laid down in such work.

(3) If its strength or purity falls below the professed standard under which it is sold or offered or exposed for sale.

(*g*) Provided, that the foregoing definitions as to the adulteration of food and drugs shall not apply—

(1) If any matter or ingredient not injurious to health has been added to the food or drug because the same is required for the production or preparation thereof as an article of commerce, in a state fit for carriage or consumption, and not fraudulently to increase the bulk, weight, or measure of the food or drug or to conceal the inferior quality thereof, if such articles are distinctly labeled as a mixture, in conspicuous characters, forming an inseparable part of the general label, which shall also bear the name and address of the manufacturer.

(2) If the food or drug is a proprietary medicine, or is the subject of a patent in force, and is supplied in the state required by the specification of the patent.

(3) If the food or drug is unavoidably mixed with some extraneous matter in the process of collection or preparation.

(4) If any articles of food not injurious to the health of the person consuming the same are mixed together and sold or offered for sale as a compound, and if such articles are distinctly labeled as a mixture, in conspicuous characters, forming an inseparable part of the general label, which shall also bear the name and address of the manufacturer.

(*h*) Every agricultural fertilizer shall be deemed to be "adulterated" within the meaning of this act if, when sold, offered, or exposed for sale, the chemical analysis thereof shows a deficiency of more than one per cent. of any of the chemical substances, the percentages whereof are required to be specified in the certificate, by "*the fertilizers act*" required to be affixed to each barrel, box, sack, or package containing the same, or (if the agricultural fertilizer is in bulk) to be produced to the inspector; or if it contains less than the minimum percentage of such substances required by the said act to be contained in such fertilizer. 48–49 V., c. 67, s. 2.

ANALYSIS.

3. The governor in council may appoint one or more persons possessing competent medical, chemical, and microscopical knowledge as analysts of food, drugs, and agricultural fertilizers purchased, sold, or exposed or offered for sale within such territorial limits as are assigned to each of them respectively, and may also select from among the aforesaid analysts so appointed, or may appoint, in addition thereto, a chief analyst, who shall be attached to the staff of the department of inland revenue at Ottawa.

(2) No analyst shall be appointed until he has undergone an examination before a special examining board appointed by the governor in council, and until he has obtained from such board a certificate setting forth that he is duly qualified to perform the duties attached to the office of analyst. 48–49 V., c. 67, s. 3; 49 V., c. 41, s. 1.

4. The governor in council may cause such remuneration to be paid to such chief analyst and to such analysts as he deems proper, and such remuneration, whether by fees, or salary, or partly in one way, and partly in the other, may be paid to them out of any sums voted by Parliament for the purposes of this act. 48–49 V., c. 67, s. 4.

5. The officers of inland revenue, the inspectors and deputy inspectors of weights and measures, and the inspectors and deputy inspectors acting under "*the general inspection act*," or any of them, shall, when required so to do by any regulation made in that behalf by the minister of inland revenue, procure and submit samples of food, drugs, or agricultural fertilizers suspected to be adulterated, to be analyzed by the analysts appointed under this act. 48–49 V., c. 67, s. 5.

6. The council of any city, town, county, or village may appoint one or more inspectors of food, drugs, and agricultural fertilizers; and such inspectors shall, for the purposes of this act, have all the powers by this act vested in officers of inland revenue; and any such inspector may require any public analyst to analyze any sam-

ples of food, drugs, or agricultural fertilizers collected by him, if such samples have been collected in accordance with the requirements of this act.

(2) The said analyst shall, upon tender of the fees fixed for the analysis of such class of articles by the governor in council, forthwith analyze the same, and give the inspector a certificate of such analysis.

(3) Such inspector may prosecute any person manufacturing, selling, or offering or exposing for sale within the city, county, town, or village for which he is appointed inspector, any article of food, drug, or agricultural fertilizer which has been certified by any public analyst to have been adulterated within the meaning of this act.

(4) Notwithstanding any other provision of this act in respect of the disposition of penalties, all penalties imposed and recovered at the suit of any such inspector shall be paid into the revenue of the city, county, town, or village by the council of which such inspector was appointed, and may be distributed in such manner as the council of such city, county, town, or village by by-law directs. 48-49 V., c. 67, s. 6.

7. Any officer may procure samples of food, drugs, or agricultural fertilizers which have not been declared exempt from the provisions of this act, from any person who has such articles in his possession for the purpose of sale, or who sells or exposes the same for sale; and he may procure such samples either by purchasing the same or by requiring the person in whose possession they are to show him and allow him to inspect all such articles in his possession, and the place or places in which such articles are stored, and to give him samples of such articles, on payment or tender of the value of such samples. 48-49 V., c. 67, s. 7.

8. If the person who has such articles in his possession, or his agent or servant, refuses or fails to admit the officer, or refuses or omits to show all or any of the said articles in his possession, or the place in which any such articles are stored, or to permit the officers to inspect the same, or to give any samples thereof, or to furnish the officer with such light or assistance as he requires, when required so to do in pursuance of this act, he shall be liable to the same penalty as if he knowingly sold or exposed for sale adulterated articles knowing them to be adulterated. 48-49 V., c. 67, s. 8.

9. The officer purchasing any article with the intention of submitting the same to be analyzed, shall, after the purchase has been completed, forthwith notify the seller or his agent selling the article of his intention to have the same analyzed by the public analyst, and shall, except in specific cases, respecting which provision is made by the governor in council, divide the article into three parts—to be then and there separated, and each part to be marked and sealed up, as its nature permits—and shall deliver one of the parts to the seller or his agent, if required by him so to do.

(2) He shall transmit another of such parts to the minister of inland revenue for submission to the chief anaylist in case of appeal, and shall submit the remaining part to the analyst for the district within which the samples were taken, unless otherwise directed by the minister of inland revenue. 48-49 V., c. 67, s. 9.

10. The person from whom any sample is obtained under this act may require the officer obtaining it to annex to the vessel or package containing the part of the sample which he is hereby required to transmit to the minister of inland revenue the name and address of such person, and to secure, with a seal or seals belonging to him, the vessel or package containing such part of the sample, and the address annexed thereto, in such manner that the vessel or package cannot be opened, or the name and address taken off, without breaking such seals; and the certificate of the chief analyst shall state the name and address of the person from whom the said sample was obtained, that the vessel or package was not open, and that the seals, securing to the vessel or package the name and address of such person, were not broken until such time as he opened the vessel or package for the purpose of making his analysis; and in such case no certificate shall be receivable in evidence, unless there is contained therein such statement as above, or a statement to the like effect. 48-49 V., c. 67, s. 10.

11. When the officer has, by either of the means aforesaid, procured samples of the articles to be analyzed, he shall cause the same to be analyzed by one of the analysts appointed under this act, and if it appears to the analyst that the sample is adulterated within the meaning of this act, he shall certify such fact, stating in such certificate, in the case of an article of food or a drug, whether such adulteration is of a nature injurious to the health of the person consuming the same; and the certificate so given shall be received as evidence in any proceedings taken against any person in pursuance of this act, subject to the right of any person against whom proceedings are taken to require the attendance of the analyst, for the purpose of cross-examination. 48–49 V., c. 67, s. 11.

12. If the vendor of the article respecting which such certificate is given deems himself aggrieved thereby, he may, within forty-eight hours of the receipt of the first notification of the intention of the officer or other purchaser to take proceedings against him (whether such notification is given by the purchaser or by the ordinary process of law), notify the said officer or purchaser in writing that he intends to appeal from the decision of the analyst to the judgment of the chief analyst: and in such case the officer or purchaser shall transmit such notification to the chief analyst, and the chief analyst shall, with all convenient speed, analyze the part of the sample transmitted to the minister of inland revenue for that purpose, and shall report thereon to the said minister; and the decision of such chief analyst shall be final, and his certificate thereof shall have the same effect as the certificate of the analyst in the next preceding section mentioned. 48–49 V., c. 67, s. 12.

13. Every analyst appointed under this act shall report quarterly to the minister of inland revenue the number of articles of food, drugs, and agricultural fertilizers analyzed by him under this act during the preceding quarter, and shall specify the nature and kind of adulterations detected in such articles of food, drugs, and agricultural fertilizers; and all such reports, or a synopsis of them, and the names of the vendors or persons from whom obtained, and of the manufacturers when known, shall be printed and laid before Parliament as an appendix to the annual report of the said minister. 48–49 V., c. 67, s. 13.

ADULTERATION.

14. No person shall manufacture, expose or offer for sale, or sell any food, drug, or agricultural fertilizer which is adulterated within the meaning of this act. 48–49 V., c. 67, s. 14.

15. If milk is sold, or offered or exposed for sale, after any valuable constituent of the article has been abstracted therefrom, or if water has been added thereto, or if it is the product of a diseased animal fed upon unwholesome food, it shall be deemed to have been adulterated in a manner injurious to health, and such sale, offer, or exposure for sale shall render the vendor liable to the penalty hereinafter provided in respect to the sale of adulterated food; except that skimmed milk may be sold as such if contained in cans bearing upon their exterior, within twelve inches of the tops of such vessels, the word "skimmed" in letters of not less than two inches in length, and served in measures also similarly marked; but any person supplying such skimmed milk, unless such quality of milk has been asked for by the purchaser, shall not be entitled to plead the provisions of this section as a defense to or in extenuation of any violation of this act:

(2) Nothing in this section shall be interpreted to permit or warrant the admixture of water with milk, or any other process than the removal of cream by skimming. 48–49 V., c. 67, s. 15.

16. Vinegar sold, or offered or exposed for sale, shall be deemed to be adulterated in a manner injurious to health if any mineral acid has been added thereto, or if it contains any soluble salt having copper or lead as a base thereof—whether such mineral acid or salt is added either during the process of manufacture or subsequently. 48–49 V., c. 67, s. 16.

17. Alcoholic, fermented, or other potable liquors sold, or offered or exposed for sale, shall be deemed to have been adulterated in a manner injurious to health if they are found to contain any of the articles mentioned in the schedule of this act, or any article hereafter added to such schedule by the governor in council. 48–49 V., c. 67, s. 17.

18. The governor in council may from time to time declare certain articles or preparations exempt in whole or in part from the provisions of this act, and may add to the schedule to this act any article or ingredient the addition of which is by him deemed necessary in the public interest; and every order in council in that behalf shall be published in the Canada Gazette, and shall take effect at the expiration of thirty days from the date of such publication. (48–49 V., c. 67 s 18.)

19. The governor in council shall from time to time cause to be prepared and published lists of the articles, mixtures, or compounds declared exempt from the provisions of this act in accordance with the next preceding section, and shall also from time to time fix the limits of variability permissible in any article of food or drug or compound the standard of which is not established by any such pharmacopœia or standard work as is hereinbefore mentioned; and the orders in council fixing the same shall be published in the Canada Gazette, and shall take effect at the expiration of thirty days after the publication thereof. (48–49 V., c. 67, s. 19.)

20. Whenever any article of food, any drug, or any agricultural fertilizer is reported by any analyst as being adulterated within the meaning of this act, the minister of inland revenue may, if he thinks fit, order such article, and all other articles of the same kind and quality which were in the same place at the time the article analyzed was obtained, to be seized by any officer of customs or inland revenue, and detained by him until an analysis of samples of the whole is made by the chief analyst. (48, 49 V., c. 67, s. 20.)

21. If the chief analyst reports to the minister of inland revenue that the whole or any part of such articles are adulterated, the minister may declare such articles, or so much thereof as the chief analyst reports as being adulterated, to be forfeited to the Crown; and such articles shall thereupon be disposed of as the minister directs. (48–49 V., c. 67, s. 21.

PENALTIES.

22. Every person who willfully adulterates any article of food or any drug, or orders any other person so to do, shall—

(*a*) If such adulteration is within the meaning of this act deemed to be injurious to health, for the first offense incur a penalty not exceeding fifty dollars and not less than ten dollars and costs, and for each subsequent offense a penalty not exceeding two hundred dollars and not less than fifty dollars and costs.

(*b*) If such adulteration is within the meaning of this act deemed not to be injurious to health, incur a penalty not exceeding thirty dollars and costs, and for each subsequent offense a penalty not exceeding one hundred dollars and not less than fifty dollars and costs. (49–49 V., c. 67, s. 22.)

23. Every person who, by himself or his agent, sells, offers for sale, or exposes for sale any article of food or any drug which is adulterated within the meaning of this act shall—

(*a*) If such adulteration is within the meaning of this act deemed to be injurious to health, for a first offense incur a penalty not exceeding fifty dollars and costs, and for each subsequent offense a penalty not exceeding two hundred dollars and not less than fifty dollars and costs.

(*b*) If such adulteration is within the meaning of this act deemed not to be injurious to health, incur for each such offsense a penalty not exceeding fifty dollars and not less than five dollars and costs.

(2) *Provided*, That if the person accused proves to the court before which the case is tried that he did not know of the article being adulterated, and shows that he could not, with reasonable diligence, have obtained that knowledge, he shall be sub-

ject only to the liability to forfeiture under the twenty-first section of this act. (48-49 V., c. 67, s. 23.)

24. Every compounder or dealer in and every manufacturer of intoxicating liquors who has in his possession or in any part of the premises occupied by him as such any adulterated liquor, knowing it to be adulterated, or any deleterious ingredient specified in the schedule hereto, or added to such schedule by the governor in council, for the possession of which he is unable to account to the satisfaction of the court before which the case is tried, shall be deemed knowingly to have exposed for sale adulterated food, and shall incur for the first offense a penalty not exceeding one hundred dollars, and for each subsequent offense a penalty not exceeding four hundred dollars. (48-49 V., c. 67, s. 24.)

25. Every person who knowingly attaches to any article of food or any drug any label which falsely describes the article sold or offered or exposed for sale, shall incur a penalty not exceeding one hundred dollars and not less than twenty dollars and costs. (48-49 V., c. 67, s. 25.)

26. Every penalty imposed and recovered under this act shall, except as herein otherwise provided, and except in the case of any suit, action, or prosecution brought or instituted under the provisions of the next following section, be paid over to the minister of finance and receiver-general, and shall form part of the consolidated revenue fund. (48-49 V., c. 67, s. 26.)

GENERAL PROVISIONS.

27. Nothing herein contained shall be held to preclude any person from submitting any sample of food, drug, or agricultural fertilizer for analysis to any public analyst, or from prosecuting the vendor thereof, if such article is found to be adulterated, but the burden of proof of sale, and of the fact that the sample was not tampered with after purchase, shall be upon the person so submitting the same:

(2) Any public analyst shall analyze such sample on payment of the fee prescribed in respect of such article or class of article by the governor in council. (48-49 V., c. 67, s. 27.)

28. Any expenses incurred in analyzing any food, drug, or agricultural fertilizer, in pursuance of this act, shall, if the person from whom the sample is taken is convicted of having in his possession, selling, offering or exposing for sale, adulterated food, drugs, or agricultural fertilizers, in violation of this act, be deemed to be a portion of the cost of the proceedings against him, and shall be paid by him accordingly; and in all other cases such expenses shall be paid as part of the expenses of the officer, or by the person who procured the sample, as the case may be. (48-49 V., c. 67, s. 28.)

29. The governor in council may, from time to time, make such regulations as to him seem necessary, for carrying the provisions of this act into effect. (48-49 V., c. 67, s. 29.)

30. The provisions of "the inland revenue act," whether enacted with special reference to any particular business or trade, or with general reference to the collection of the revenue, or the prevention, detection, or punishment of fraud or neglect in relation thereto, shall extend, apply, and be construed, and shall have effect with reference to this act, as if they had been enacted with special reference to the matters and things herein provided for.

(2) Every penalty imposed under this act may be enforced and dealt with as if imposed under the said act, and every compounder, and the apparatus used by him, and the place in which his business is carried on, and the articles made or compounded by him, or used in compounding any such article, shall be "subject to excise" under the said act. (48-49 V., c. 67, s. 30.)

SCHEDULE.

Cocculus indicus, chloride of sodium (otherwise common salt), copperas, opium, cayenne pepper, picric acid, Indian hemp, strychnine, tobacco, darnel seed, extract of logwood, salts of zinc, copper, or lead, alum, methyl alcohol and its derivatives, amyl alcohol, and any extract or compound of any of the above ingredients.

The English laws will be found in Hassall or Blyth.

INDEX

A

B.

C.

Page.

D.

E.

F.

G.

H.

J.

L.

M.

○

Fig 25

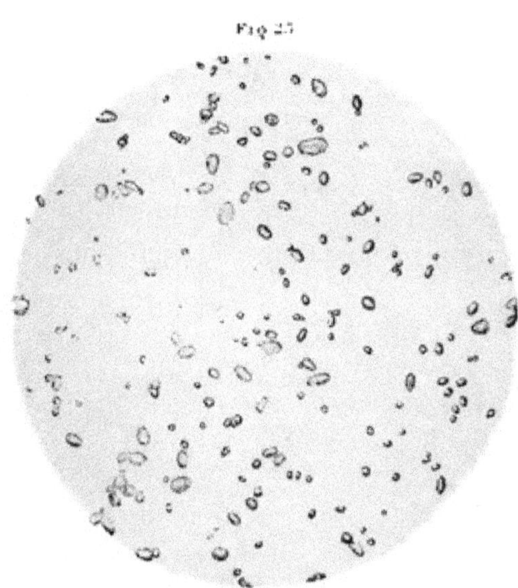

STARCH PLAIN ILLUMINATION x 43

Fig 26

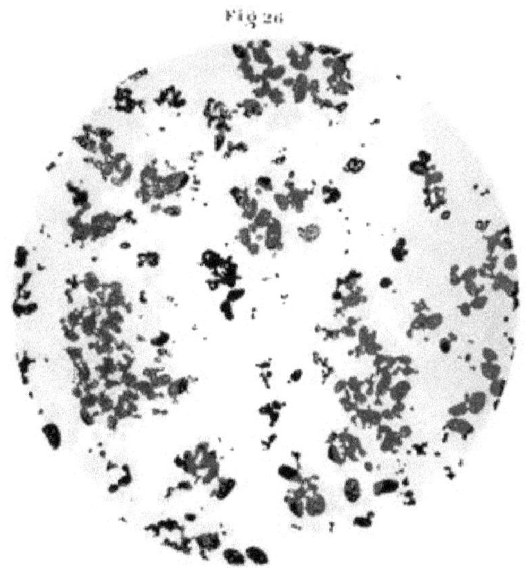

STARCH STAINED WITH IODINE x 43

Photo by Clifford Richardson A. Hoen & Co. Heliocaustic Baltimore

Fig. 27

MARANTA STARCH

Fig. 28

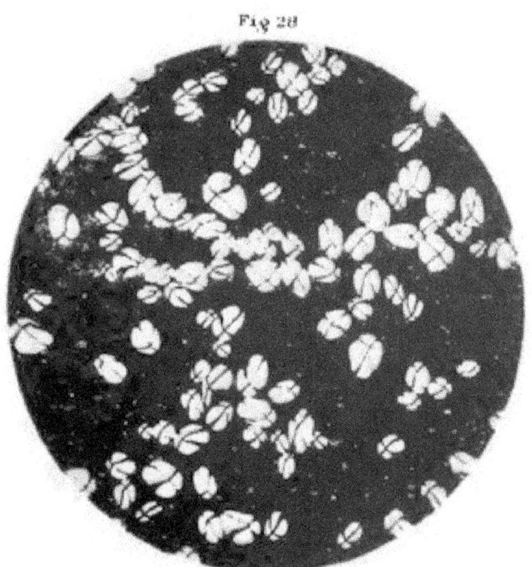

MARANTA STARCH x140

Photo. by Clifford Richardson. A. Hoen & Co. Heliocaustic Baltimore

Fig 29

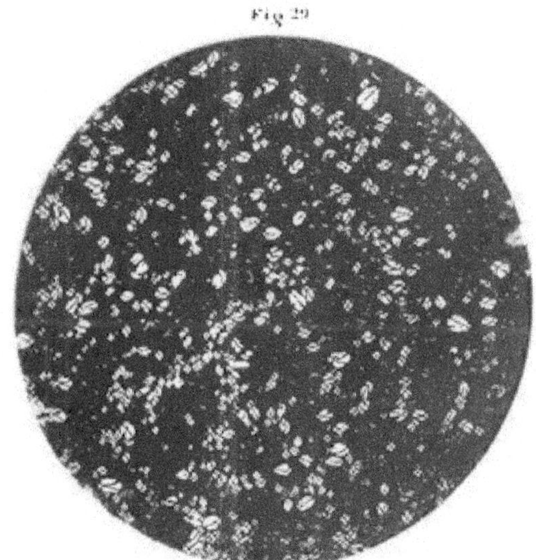

POTATO STARCH x 43

Fig 30

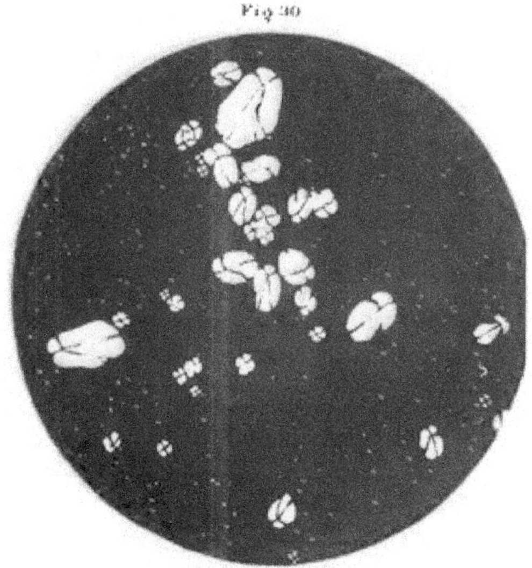

POTATO STARCH

Fig 31

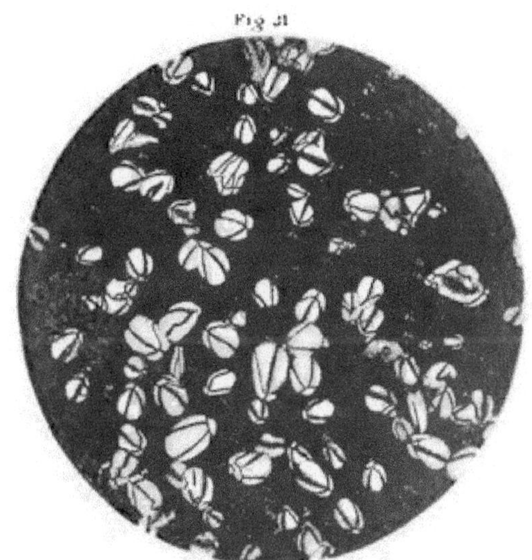

POTATO STARCH x 144

Fig 32

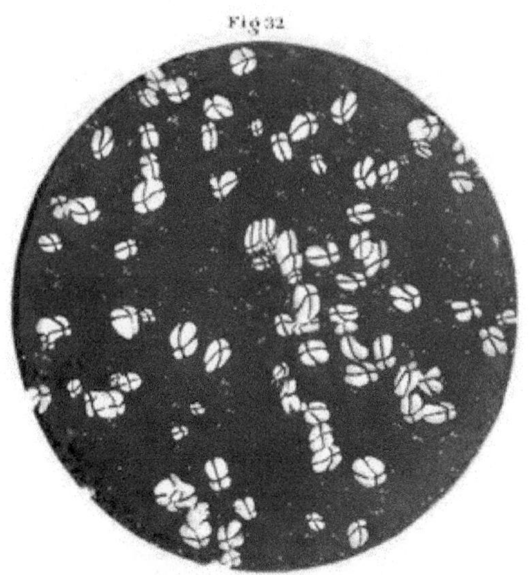

MARANTA STARCH x 144

Photo by Clifford Richardson

A. Hoen & Co. Heliocaustic, Baltimore

Fig 33

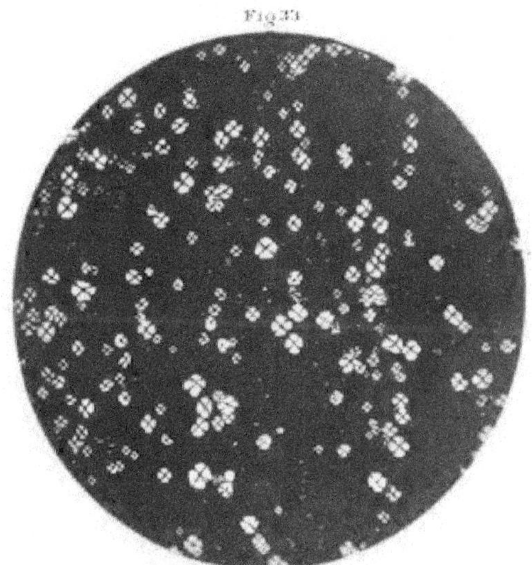

MAIZE STARCH x145

Fig 34

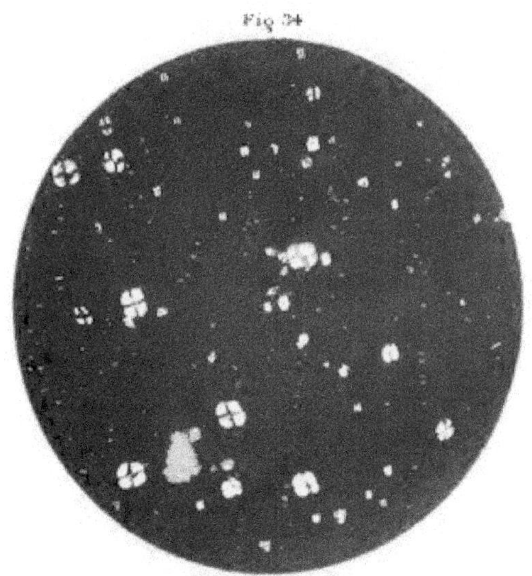

WHEAT STARCH x145

Photo by Clifford Richardson A. Hoen & Co. Lithocaustic Baltimore

Fig. 35

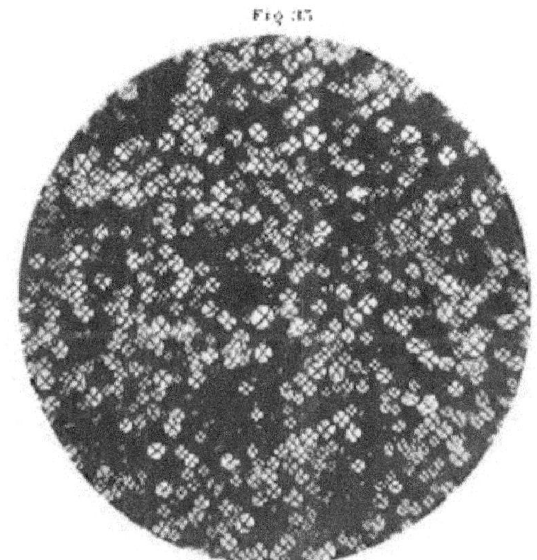

RICE STARCH x150

Fig. 36

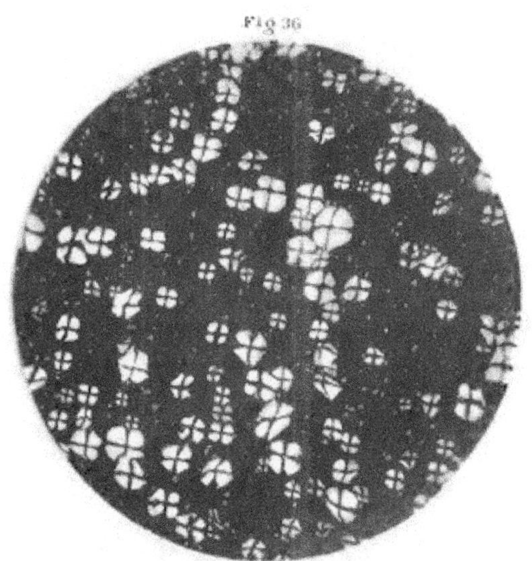

RICE STARCH x450

Photo. by Clifford Richardson

A. Hoen & Co. Heliocaustic, Baltimore

Fig. 37

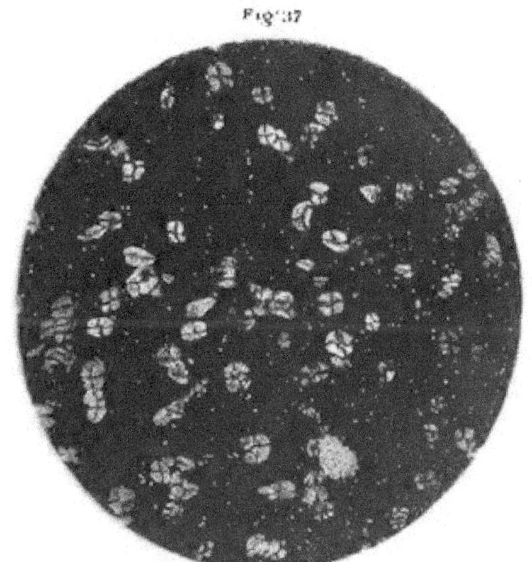

BARLEY STARCH x150

Fig. 38

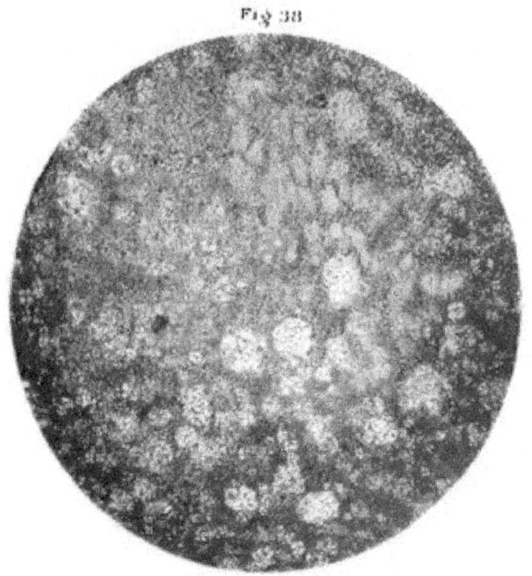

OAT STARCH x160

Photo. by Clifford Richardson.

A. Hoen & Co. Heliocaustic, Baltimore

Fig. 39

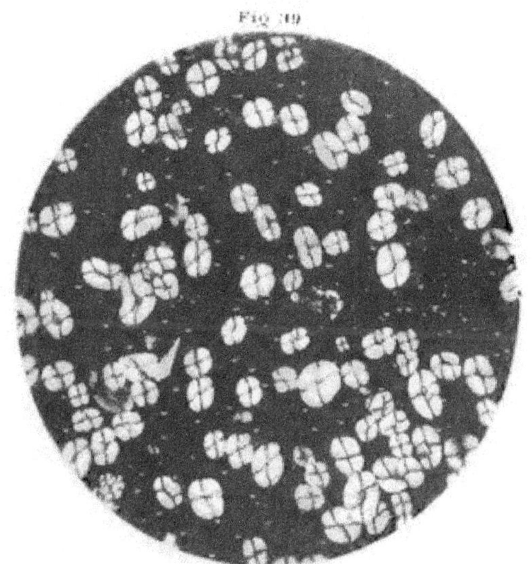

BEAN STARCH x145

Fig. 40

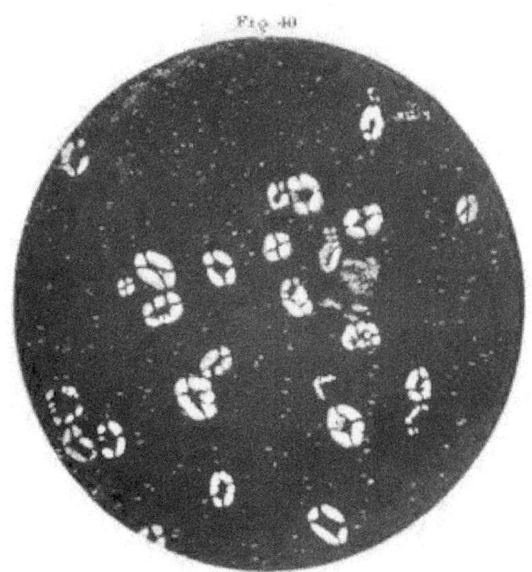

PEA STARCH x145

Photo by Clifford Richardson

A. Hoen & Co. Heliocaustic Baltimore

Fig 41

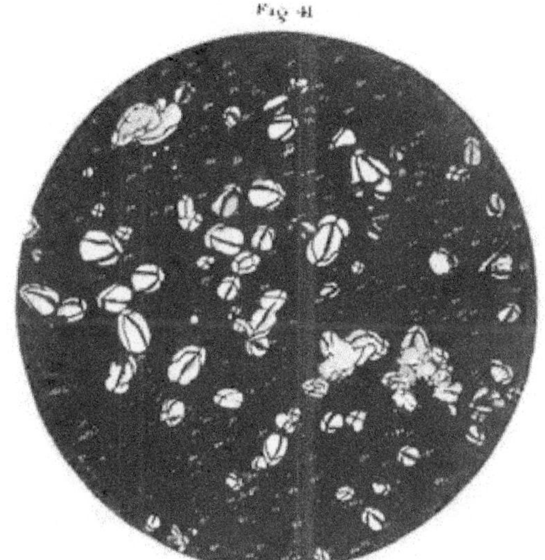

GINGER STARCH x145

Fig 42

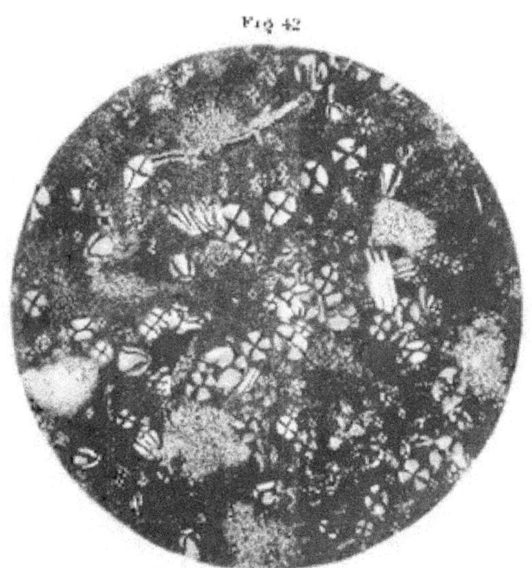

GINGER ADULTERATED x145

Photo by Clifford Richardson

A. Hoen & Co. Heliocaustic Baltimore

Fig 43

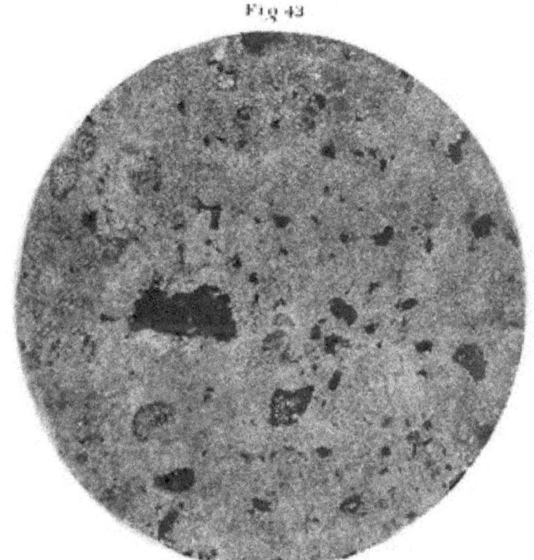

BLACK PEPPER P.D. x 45

Fig 44

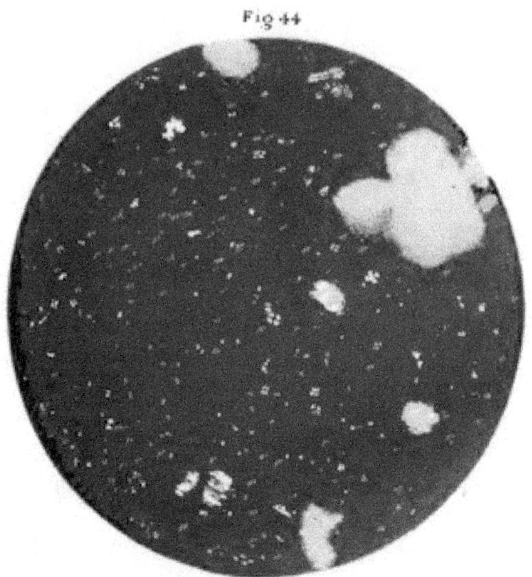

PEPPER ADULTERATED x 45

Photo by Clifford Richardson. A Hoen & Co. Lithocaustic, Baltimore

Fig. 45

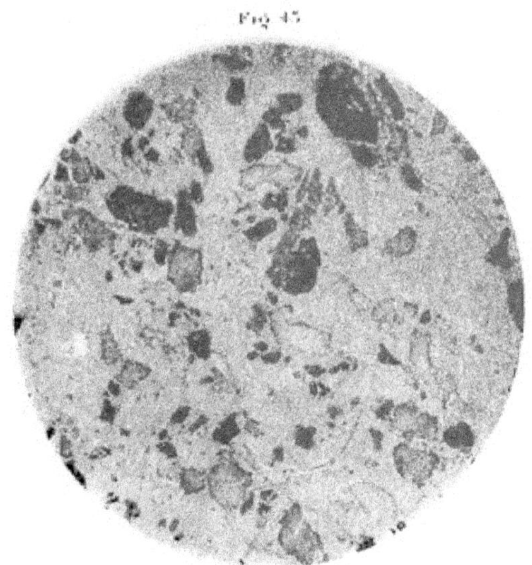

CINNAMON ADULTERATED

Photo. by Clifford Richardson

A. Hoen & Co. Heliocaustic Baltimore

Fig. 46.

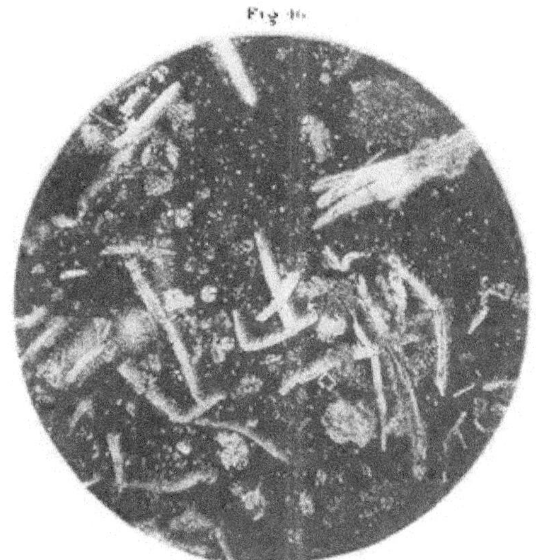

CINNAMON x 45

Fig. 47

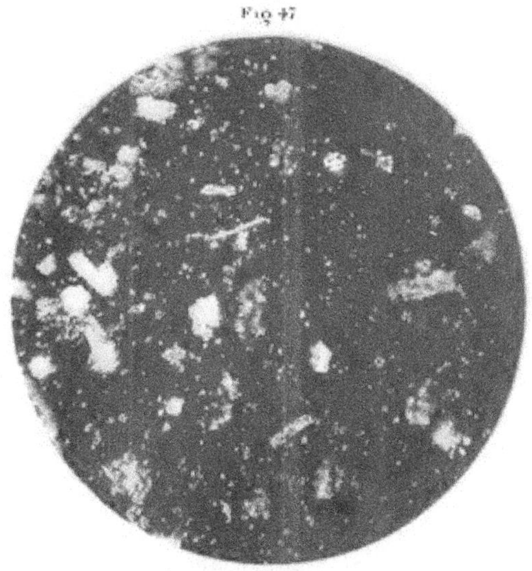

CASSIA x 45

Photo by Clifford Richardson

A. Hoen & Co. Lithocaustic Baltimore

Fig 48

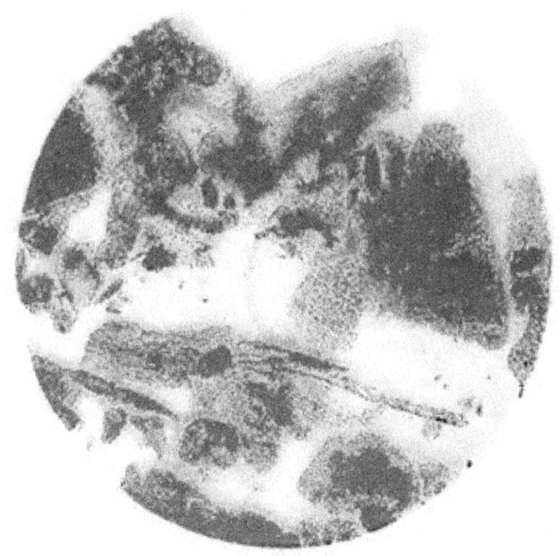

CAYENNE

Fig 49

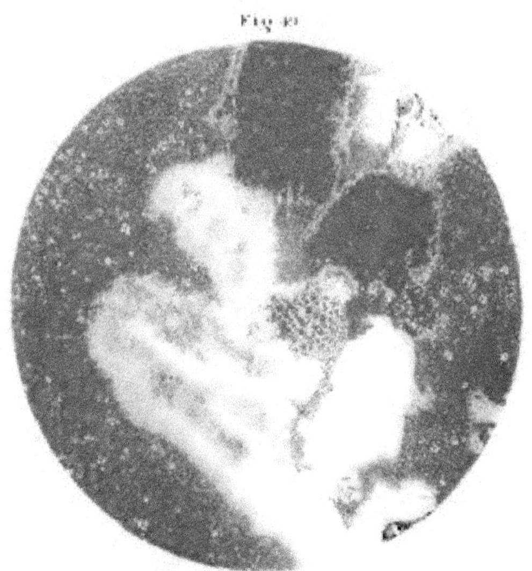

CAYENNE ADULTERATED

Photo by Clifford Richardson

A Hoen & Co [illegible] Baltimore

www.ingramcontent.com/pod-product-compliance
Lightning Source LLC
Chambersburg PA
CBHW020556270326
41927CB00006B/861

* 9 7 8 3 3 3 7 2 0 1 1 3 5 *